Productivity and the Law

Productivity is a goal achieved only by contented employees

Louis Martin, JD

Productivity and the Law

Productivity is a goal achieved only by contented employees

Copyright © 2015 by Louis Martin

HRComplianceTraining.Net
6145 North Sheridan Road – Suite 20B
Chicago, IL 60660

First Edition: June, 2015

Productivity and the Law: a book by Louis Martin
ISBN-13: 978-0692464137

Created in the United States of America

This book is dedicated to my wife, Vikki Ward Martin, BA, MA and M. Div., who has been my life partner for more than a quarter century.

With Vikki's love, support, and understanding I have been able to travel far and wide to develop and deliver Leader-Led Employment Law Training Seminars to hundreds of employers and thousands of employees.

Thank you, dear Vikki; I couldn't have done it without you.

Louis

ABOUT THE AUTHOR

Attorney Louis Martin and HRComplianceTraining.Net associates have trained hundreds of employers, training thousands of employees in the areas of Leadership of People, Management of Processes, HR Legal Compliance, Workplace Diversity/Inclusion and Work/Life Enhancement.

A skilled human resource development trainer and consultant, Attorney Martin is involved day-to-day as one of HRComplianceTraining.Net's expert training team members, serves on the faculty of the American Management Association, and has been engaged in the practice of law for over 40 years.

A graduate of the University Of Iowa College Of Law, Martin served as a Reginald Heber Smith Community Fellow, a partner in the law firm of Mahon and Martin, an executive for civil rights enforcement in Connecticut, Iowa, and Maryland, and has also served as an administrative law judge.

For more information, visit **www.hrcompliancetraining.net**

CONTENTS

FOREWORD

INTRODUCTION

PART I – PRODUCTIVITY AND COMPLIANCE

Chapter 1	Productivity and compliance . . . partners in profitability	2
Chapter 2	Employment law compliance and your value proposition	6
Chapter 3	HR today . . . a profit center	11
Chapter 4	How employment laws help you help your bottom line	13
Chapter 5	Increase your contribution to the bottom line through HR compliance training	16

PART II – THE ESSENTIAL LAWS

Chapter 6	Essential employment laws	20
Chapter 7	A thumbnail sketch of the U.S. Equal Employment Opportunity Commission (EEOC)	24
Chapter8	The Affordable Care Act (ACA) . . . the basics and a link you can count on	26
Chapter 9	The Americans with Disabilities Act (ADA)	30
Chapter 10	The Fair Labor Standards Act (FLSA)	35
Chapter 11	The Family and Medical Leave Act (FMLA)	37
Chapter 12	How the Family and Medical Leave Act (FMLA) gave an eternal gift to a mother and daughter	42
Chapter 13	Employee misclassification . . . what can it cost?	45
Chapter 14	How to keep up with complex employment laws and regulations	49

PART III – DISCRIMINATION

Chapter 15	The most expensive ($160 million) employment law violation in history didn't have to happen	54
Chapter 16	Could an age discrimination lawsuit put you out of business?	57

PART IV – HARASSMENT

Chapter 17	Sexual harassment and you	62
Chapter 18	How to investigate an allegation of sexual harassment	66
Chapter 19	Workplace harassment and you	73
Chapter 20	An example of harassment unchecked (based on an actual event)	76

PART V – MANAGING AND THE LAW

Chapter 21	How to construct HR policies to protect employees, profits, and personal and professional reputations	81
Chapter 22	What is an HR audit and why should you care?	84
Chapter 23	Department of Labor (DOL) investigators are on the way . . . what now?	87
Chapter 24	Employment "at-will" . . . what does it mean?	92
Chapter 25	Constructive Discharge . . . what does it really mean?	95
Chapter 26	Progressive employee discipline – your best insurance policy?	98
Chapter 27	You, employee performance logs, and the law	103
Chapter 28	HR recruiting and interviewing checklist	108
Chapter 29	On-site employment law training . . . yes, no, maybe?	113
Chapter 30	How to choose the right HR compliance trainer	116
Chapter 31	How to generate a return on your investment in employment law compliance training	118
Chapter 32	The best HR compliance policy is common sense (but you already knew that, didn't you?)	121
Chapter 33	Keep up to keep yourself and your organization out of court	124

PART VI – EEOC RULINGS

Chapter 34	Who is the EEOC and why should you care?	128
Chapter 35	Wal-Mart to Pay $150,000 to settle EEOC age and disability discrimination suit	131

Chapter 36   KMART will pay $102,048 to settle EEOC disability discrimination lawsuit   **135**

Chapter 37   Citicorp ordered to pay nearly $340,000 for violating the Equal Pay Act   **140**

Chapter 38   EEOC sues BNV Home Care Agency for violating Genetic Information Nondiscrimination Act   **142**

Chapter 39   Seapod Pawnshops to pay $300,000 to settle EEOC harassment lawsuit   **145**

Chapter 40   Swift Aviation to pay $50,000 to settle EEOC national origin and religious discrimination lawsuit   **149**

Chapter 41   Savi Technology will pay $20,000 to settle EEOC pregnancy discrimination lawsuit   **152**

Chapter 42   Kauai County in Hawaii settles EEOC race harassment suit for $120,000   **156**

Chapter 43   Kentucky Fried Chicken franchise pays $40,000 to settle EEOC religious discrimination lawsuit   **159**

Chapter 44   Jury awards $499,000 against EmCare in EEOC sexual harassment and retaliation case   **162**

Chapter 45   Ventura corporation to pay $354,250 to settle EEOC lawsuit for sex discrimination against men   **166**

Chapter 46   Jury awards more than $1.5 million in EEOC sexual harassment and retaliation suit against New Breed Logistics   **170**

Chapter 47   After 44 years, sheet metal union finally agrees to pay an estimated $12 million in the partial settlement of race bias lawsuit   **174**

Appendix   The major federal employment laws   **179**

FOREWORD

I wrote this book to offer my decades of experience as an employment law attorney and seminar facilitator to help you make the most of the connection between employment law compliance and three critical benefits for you and your organization: 1. Improved workplace harmony, 2. Increased productivity and profitability, and, 3. Reduced potential for individual and organizational legal liabilities.

This book can be a useful guide you can rely on to help you create, develop, and sustain harmonious, productive employer/employee relationships in your workplace.

I encourage you to keep the following facts in mind about this book. This is not a law book . . . law books are for lawyers. This book contains general information and guidelines and is not intended to address every possible employment law issue.

The strategies and tactics described in this book may be modified or updated over time and we will include any changes in subsequent revisions.

I hope you enjoy your reading experience and look forward to hearing about your personal and professional successes as you navigate the life cycle of employment.

Sincerely,

Louis Martin, JD

INTRODUCTION

This book will take you on a step-by-step journey through the life cycle of employment and will introduce you to the skills you need to not only successfully navigate human resources challenges you encounter each and every day but to also comply with the employment laws and regulations that can put you and your organization at risk.

Managing people in the workplace is one of the toughest jobs on the planet and I would ask anyone who doubts that assertion to consider the following daunting facts:

- More than one-quarter of all civil lawsuits filed in this country are employment related
- Employers lose approximately 60% of all such lawsuits
- Employees sue not only their employers . . . they sue directors, executives, HR professionals, key personnel, managers, and supervisors who can be held personally liable for legal costs and court awards
- Courts typically award $500,000.00 or more to sexual harassment plaintiffs
- Most employer-defendants, regardless of size or economic strength, spend more than $100,000.00 to defend a sexual harassment lawsuit

When people who work together come into conflict, productivity and profitability are put at risk until a permanent resolution is in place.

Timely, proactive conflict resolution is simply good business . . . for employees, for employers, for suppliers, for vendors, and, especially, for clients.

If you're willing to invest time and effort into recognizing, understanding, and applying the strategies and tactics presented in this book, you can learn how to effectively negotiate creative, viable resolutions to current and future workplace conflicts.

At the end of the day, who could ask for anything more?

I – PRODUCTIVITY AND COMPLIANCE

Chapter 1
Productivity and compliance . . . partners in profitability

IS IT TRUE?

Is productivity not a hope but a goal achieved only by contented employees?

Most employers are keenly aware of a singularly disturbing fact . . . too many employees don't feel appreciated or understood and are therefore unable or unwilling to make an all-out commitment to supporting the employer's mission.

Productive employers . . . *for-profit, not-for-profit, private or public* . . . understand that the best way to develop and sustain a contented workforce is to comply with applicable local, state, and federal employment laws.

So, the question that begs to be answered is, how can an employer motivate employees to become fully engaged in accomplishing the organization's mission?

There is a 3-part integrated answer to that question:

1. Senior management must effectively define and communicate the organization's mission to all employees.
2. Supervisory personnel must encourage and sustain open, viable, give-and-take relationships with employees.
3. Senior management and supervisory personnel must create a safe, secure, balanced, harmonious workplace to promote each employee's sense of devotion to and pride in the organization's mission.

Senior management and supervisory personnel can provide the following tools to apply that 3-part answer:

- Quality in-house or out-sourced employment law training designed to promote workplace harmony. Employment law compliance training must objectively serve the unique aspects of each employer's specific culture and productivity challenges and opportunities.
- Recognition that employees are strongly motivated by money. Money is, after all, a primary reason most people get up every day to go to work and management should intelligently and fairly provide

Productivity and the Law
Louis Martin, JD
Productivity is a goal achieved only by contented employees

meaningful financial incentives to motivate productive employees in all pay grades.

- Constant awareness of the intrinsic value of meaningful feedback. People are people and every person wants to feel good about the work he or she does. It is therefore essential to train key personnel, line managers, supervisors, and senior management to provide regular, honest, positive feedback to encourage all employees, including even the newest, least productive workers to reach new plateaus of productivity and profitability.

- Respect for employees not only as workers but also as human beings. It goes without saying that an employee who feels respected by his or her employer is more likely to do whatever they can to help the organization to fulfill its mission.

- The same 'productivity training' for key personnel, line managers, and supervisors as senior management receives. It is especially important to provide 'productivity training' to manager-candidates and to new managers. Productivity training should include:
  - How to focus one's attention on the task at hand.

4 |

- How to successfully integrate commitments, information, and communication into achieving specific goals.
- How to get the most out of electronic and software resources.
- How to be proactive, not reactive, when faced with challenges and opportunities.
- Stand by employees whenever they need support. Support for employees can be expressed in a number of ways: By providing the essential tools and resources they need to perform their jobs; by getting to know who they are, where they are, and what they want to do; and by ensuring that each employee has consistent opportunities to achieve and maintain a reasonable professional/personal life balance.

The record is clear . . . thousands upon thousands of employers across the nation who invest in employment law training and provide the tools outlined here, profit substantially from the added efforts of motivated employees who are significantly more engaged in their jobs and are therefore much more productive.

Chapter 2
Employment law compliance and your value proposition

JOAN CARTER*, SALES MANAGER for a nationally known retailer, was perplexed. As the economy recovered from the Great Recession, increasing numbers of experienced sales staff left for better paying jobs with larger companies in various industries, forcing her to hire inexperienced replacements.

The influx of new trainees led to dysfunctional sales team dynamics, a lack of engagement with customers, and resulted in a 20-plus percent drop in sales, prompting Joan to ask the big question faced by every retailer in a similar situation: *What can I do to turn around a precipitous drop in sales and how quickly can I do it?*

As Joan thought about it, she concluded that she could find the solution in a straightforward answer to a single, simple question: *What motivates any customer to buy from us?*

6 |

Joan realized that the best way to get a useful answer to that question would be to contact a significant sampling of paying customers for at least the past six months . . . and that is precisely what she did; day after day for more than a month.

And, after talking to more than a hundred current and past customers, what did Joan learn?

She learned what she already knew . . . that while people buy to fulfill real or perceived needs and want ease-of-use, quality, prestige, price, and/or security, they are almost always willing to drop any or all of those requirements to buy from someone who freely and sincerely expresses appreciation for their business.

So, the summary question that begs to be answered for Joan and for anyone who sells any product or service is, *how can you simultaneously fulfil a buyer's need while making that person feel good about buying from you?*

Embedded in the answer to that question is your 'value proposition'.

Assuming that your products and services perform as advertised, how can you be sure that current and prospective customers understand and *buy* your 'value proposition'?

Whether yours is a brick and mortar business or an online enterprise or any combination thereof, your customers will, at some time during the buying process, interact, face-to-face, voice-to-voice, or click-to-click, with the employees who produce, store, sell, deliver, and guarantee your products and services. Your value proposition, therefore, is measured by how your employees care for and about your customers.

Let me repeat that because it is too important to say it only once: *Your value proposition is measured by how your employees care for and about your customers.*

So, you may be wondering, *what on earth does my value proposition have to do with employment laws?*

That's a good question . . . followed by the following good answer:

Local, state, and federal employment laws essentially require employers and employees to treat each other with dignity and respect. And, employees who are treated well are more likely to have a sense of ownership and pride in the employer's mission which motivates them to work harder to understand and promote the organization's value proposition.

Happy employees will make the effort to better understand the needs of customers who want to buy a product or service to clean a floor, shine a car, speed up internet access, etc. or to take care of one or more of

Maslow's hierarchy of basic needs . . . food, health, safety, shelter, sleep, etc.

Organizational compliance with employment laws can create a harmonious working environment in which employees will be predisposed to:

- Know customers well enough to know what specific problem(s) they need to solve and will therefore be better able to help the right person select the right product or service.
- Learn everything they will need to know about how, when, and why your products and services will more effectively meet customer needs than your competitors' products or services.
- Build stronger, longer working relationships with customers who will begin to rely on your employees to be trustworthy sources of reliable information.

If you make it your business to provide a safe, secure, respectful working environment for your employees and train them to know your customers, know their needs, and care enough to build working relationships with them, your value proposition will speak for itself.

Won't it?

*Joan Carter is a pseudonym and, if you were wondering, she was able to turn sales around, relatively quickly, after taking the following steps:

1. She decided to fix the worst problem first by hiring an employment law training consultant to help establish workplace policies which would provide a well-defined, concise framework within which experienced and inexperienced employees could begin to understand, appreciate, and cooperate with one another.

2. Joan asked each sales person to contact each paying customer to offer a sincere thank-you within 24 hours of each transaction.

Chapter 3
HR today . . . a profit center?

MIKE THOMAS* IS NEARING RETIREMENT and he's been an HR executive for more than 40 years. Mike spends a lot of time these days reminiscing about the good old days . . . when his job was so much easier . . . when HR's primary role was to simply maintain employee records and process payroll.

How about you? Do you remember the *good old days*? The good old days when marketing, sales, production, and distribution were primarily responsible for profits?

Not today. No choice.

HR today must be a profit center.

Why?

Because employment law violations can cost millions of dollars in retained profits.

Just last October, for example, a federal district court in California upheld a $4 million award to an employee who was fired in retaliation for having complained about the employer's lunch and break practices.

Productivity and the Law
Louis Martin, JD
Productivity is a goal achieved only by contented employees

$4 million . . . that's a ton of profits!

Any employer who wants to avoid winding up on the wrong end of a multi-million dollar verdict must rely on HR to make sure that the organization consistently complies with all applicable employment laws and regulations.

Is this a challenge?

Sure is . . . but so what?

Every challenge brings with it opportunity.

Through no fault of your own, your organization may be faced with major challenges . . . *a labor pool in desperate need of skilled, motivated employees, market volatility, and/or constantly changing laws and regulations* . . . challenges that can be turned into opportunities provided HR works to keep your organization compliant with local, state, and federal employment laws and regulations.

In other words, HR today can give your employees the training and insights they need to learn, adapt, and incorporate employment law compliant principles, strategies, and tactics into their day-to-day attitudes, decisions, and activities.

As always, we welcome your comments and suggestions at info@hrcompliancetraining.net.

*Mike Thomas is a pseudonym

Chapter 4
How employment laws
help you help your bottom line

IT'S AN IMMUTABLE TRUTH: Employment laws affect the personal, professional, and financial lives of millions of Americans on both sides of the employer/employee equation. It is therefore reasonable to assume that these laws, properly applied, can improve the quality of life for employees and improve productivity *and increase profits* for employers.

While we may not typically think about the employer/employee relationship this way, employment laws in America today are essentially based upon the ancient master/servant relationship with the employer cast as the master and the employee cast as the servant.

The expectation is that the servant will fulfill the master's mission by making the efforts necessary to create value in the production and delivery of products and/or services to generate revenues and profits for the master.

The master, on the other hand, is expected to justly compensate the servant for his or her efforts ("The workman is worthy of his hire").

Some masters, however, as some masters will, may abuse servants out of a sense of power and/or greed and some servants, as some servants will, may be inclined to take advantage of masters for personal gain.

Ergo, this ancient concept is the primary moving force behind employment laws (*ostensibly designed to be fair and equitable*) to protect masters from servants while simultaneously protecting servants from masters.

While it may not always seem so, employment laws are not written, interpreted, and enforced to obfuscate the master/servant relationship but to clarify that relationship and to define a meaningful balance to ensure fairness for both sides.

Employment laws prohibit employers from abusing or discriminating against employees and require employers to provide reasonable compensation for reasonable work and to also provide a safe, secure workplace for employees.

Conversely, employment laws require employees to comply with employer work rules and to make every reasonable effort to honestly, safely, and productively fulfill the duties and responsibilities of the jobs they are employed to perform.

Additionally, employment laws not only protect employers and employees, they also protect the interests of various other economic players . . . bankers, consumers, investors, and local, state and federal tax collectors . . . and are therefore essential to promoting and preserving a productive, profitable, secure economy.

Employment laws, therefore, are not just scads of ludicrous regulations jammed down the throats of America's employers by gaggles of faceless, out-of-touch bureaucrats.

Employment laws, when you think about them (as every employer should), are the essential foundation upon which a viable economy functions.

Aren't they?

Chapter 5
Increase your contribution to the bottom line through HR compliance training

"In order to be irreplaceable one must always be different".

~ Coco Chanel

IS THAT TRUE?

Did Coco have it right?

Do you have to be different to be irreplaceable?

Yes . . . because if you are willing to be different, you are more likely to have the characteristics . . . *creativity and a willingness to take risks, coupled with a strong work ethic . . .* associated with irreplaceable people in the workplace.

Different . . . like Apple's Steve Jobs, California's only 4-time Governor Jerry Brown, Chrysler's Lee Iacocca, General Electric's Jack Welch, HP's Meg Whitman, Microsoft's Bill Gates, and too many others to mention here.

What, you may ask, does being different and being irreplaceable have to do with your ability to contribute to the bottom line vis-à-vis HR compliance training?

When you proactively implement HR compliance training in your workplace, you improve employee morale, protect your organization from negative publicity, increase productivity, and you add to the bottom line not only by improving profitability but by also avoiding the fees, fines, and judgments that can result from employment lawsuits.

If that doesn't make you different and irreplaceable; or as close to being irreplaceable as you can be, I don't know what would.

It's not like you have a whole lot of choice these days.

First and foremost, employment law compliance is simply the right thing to do . . . no employee should have to put up with discrimination or harassment of any kind, on any level, in any workplace today . . . *ever!*

Secondly, the federal government and a number of states and localities are continuing to increase their efforts to enforce employment law compliance training requirements.

And, these agencies are not at all shy about exacting their pounds of flesh in the form of court ordered fines and judgments.

Don't believe it?

If you're a doubter, you should know that, by law, some agencies are authorized to unilaterally collect fines and damage awards of up to $150,000.00 from each employer or individual found guilty of in any way harassing any employee who dares to complain about an employment law violation.

The $150,000.00, by the way, is in addition to the unlimited damages a court can award to a complaining employee.

Last but not least, courts are not at all timid about awarding huge amounts of money to plaintiffs . . . to be paid by organizations and even individual managers and supervisors who are convicted of having violated employment laws.

If you have any doubt about how a court might react to employment law violations, consider the $12.7 million dollar award a sheet metal union agreed to pay in a "partial settlement" of a race bias lawsuit . . . *44 years after the fact!* (See Chapter 47 for details).

The moral of the story?

Be different, be irreplaceable, and enjoy the profits!

II – THE ESSENTIAL LAWS

Chapter 6
Essential employment laws

DEPENDENT ON SIZE (number of employees), most employers in America are legally if not morally obligated to comply with all federal employment laws.

'Essential' employment laws can make or break any employer, no matter how well-funded, no matter how well known, and no matter how large or powerful that employer might be.

For that reason, it is critical for every manager, every supervisor, and all key personnel to have a working knowledge of the following essential employment laws:

- **Anti-discrimination** . . . Employers may not discriminate against any applicant or employee because of age, disability, gender, pregnancy, or national origin, race, or religion.
  - *Penalties* . . . Employers found guilty of discrimination in the workplace are subject to

the following penalties: Fines and court awarded judgments, attorney fees and investigation and court costs, and loss of revenue, profits, and reputation. Refer to www.eeoc.gov for more information

- **Harassment . . .** According to the Department of Labor (DOL), workplace harassment is typically manifested in the following ways: 1. Quid pro quo harassment in which an employee is required to submit to an employer, manager, or supervisor to avoid an unfavorable decision or negative treatment or for a favorable employment decision or treatment and, 2. Any time an employee is subjected to humiliating, offensive, or threatening behavior and/or unwelcome advances by any other person.

  o *Penalties . . .* An employer can be required to pay compensation to a victim of any form of harassment plus fines, judgments, court costs, and legal fees. A victim of workplace harassment may even press criminal charges against a perpetrator who, if convicted, may then be sentenced to probation, to perform community service, or even to serve time in jail. Refer to www.dol.gov for more information.

- **Employee minimum wage, overtime pay, recordkeeping, and child labor . . .** Employers are required to comply with the Fair Labor Standards Act (FLSA) (Chapter 10) which establishes federal minimum wage and overtime pay standards for hourly employees. FLSA also specifies how employers are required to record employee time and pay and establishes specific requirements regarding child labor.

  - *Penalties . . .* the FLSA authorizes the Wage and Hour Division of the Department of Labor to penalize employers up to $1,100.00 for each violation of minimum wage and overtime regulations. Employers may also be held liable for lost wages plus court imposed penalties plus costs and legal fees. Refer to www.dol.gov for more information.

- **Family leave . . .** The Family and Medical Leave Act (FMLA) (Chapter 11) provides up to 12 weeks per year of job-protected unpaid leave for employees with one year of service. FMLA leave may be taken to allow an employee to care for himself or herself, to care for an ill family member, or for the adoption or birth of a child.

- o **Penalties . . .** Employers and individual supervisors can be held organizationally and/or personally liable for FMLA violations. Penalties can include actual and liquidated damages plus interest and penalties plus court costs and legal fees.

Note: Because federal employment laws and regulations are in constant flux, I cannot guarantee this list to be comprehensive and consistently current. I therefore recommend that you occasionally refer to the Department of Labor website (www.dol.gov) for updates.

Chapter 7
A thumbnail sketch of the U.S. Equal Employment Opportunity Commission (EEOC)

THE U.S. EQUAL EMPLOYMENT OPPORTUNITY COMMISSION (EEOC) is the governmental agency responsible for enforcing federal laws and regulations that make it illegal for employers with at least 15 employees (20 employees in age discrimination cases) to discriminate against job applicants and employees in any or all of the following linked categories:

- Age
- Disability
- Equal Pay/Compensation
- Genetic Information
- Harassment

- National Origin
- Pregnancy
- Race/Color
- Religion
- Retaliation
- Sex
- Sexual Harassment

The U.S. Equal Employment Opportunity Commission should be taken seriously by every serious employer.

The EEOC, after all, managed to vigorously collect nearly $1.5 billion in judgments, fines, and penalties from employers, large and small, throughout America between 1997 and 2014.

Chapter 8
The Affordable Care Act (ACA) . . . the basics and a link you can count on

THE AFFORDABLE HEALTH CARE ACT (ACA), also known as 'ObamaCare', has been the law of the land since March 23, 2010 and, among other provisions, guarantees Americans the right to access affordable health insurance coverage, protects consumers from exclusion by insurance companies for pre-existing conditions, provides tax credits to help small businesses to provide health care insurance for employees, offers free preventive services, establishes rights allowing consumers to appeal negative decisions by insurance companies, delivers arguably lower health insurance rates, and dramatically reduces prescription costs for senior citizens.

Politicians and special interest groups have attempted to obfuscate some of the provisions of the ACA . . . so, to ensure that I don't add to the confusion, please permit me to directly quote the IRS on the ACA:

"The Affordable Care Act, or health care law, contains benefits and responsibilities for employers. The size and structure of your workforce – small, large, or part of a group – helps determine what applies to you. However, if you have no employees, the following information does not apply to you.

Small employers, *generally those with fewer than 50 full-time employees, may be eligible for credits and other benefits.*

A large employer *has 50 or more full-time employees or equivalents.*

An employer's size is determined by number of employees. Employer benefits, opportunities and requirements are dependent upon the employer's size and the applicable rules. Generally, an employer with 50 or more full-time employees or equivalents will be considered a large employer.

Go to http://www.irs.gov/Affordable-Care-Act for details

Employers with:

- *Fewer than 25 full-time equivalent employees may be eligible for a Small Business Health Care Tax Credit to help cover the cost of providing coverage.*

- 50 or fewer employees may be eligible to buy coverage through the Small Business Health Options Program (SHOP). Learn more at HealthCare.gov.

- 50 or more full-time equivalent employees will need to file an annual information return reporting whether and what health insurance they offered employees. In addition, they are subject to the Employer Shared Responsibility provisions.

- Regardless of size, all employers that provide self-insured health coverage to their employees must file an annual return reporting certain information for each employee they cover.

Certain affiliated employers with common ownership or part of a controlled group must aggregate their employees to determine their workforce size. Proposed regulations and FAQs you can find at http://www.irs.gov/Affordable-Care-Act provide more information about determining the size of your workforce."

The ACA allows employers to select the best and most affordable insurance plan for their employees through federal or state-run health insurance exchanges.

Americans who don't have access to health insurance through an employer can compare health insurance providers, shop premiums, and sign-up online for coverage through these same exchanges.

Politicians, influenced by lobbyists and other forces, have attempted several times over the years to repeal and/or dilute provisions of the ACA so, because those influences can be so pervasive, I recommend that you go to http://obamacarefacts.com/obamacare-news/ to check on the current status of the ACA before making any final health care coverage decisions for yourself, your family, or your employees.

Chapter 9
The Americans with Disabilities Act (ADA)

THE AMERICANS WITH DISABILITIES ACT (ADA) was signed into law on July 26, 1990 by President George H.W. Bush to protect disabled 'qualified applicants and employees' (men and women who can perform essential job duties, with or without some type of accommodation) from employers* who:

- Discriminate for any reason against a qualified job applicant, prospective employee, or current employee with a disability

- Discriminate against an applicant, prospective employee, or current employee because that person has a relationship with a disabled person

- Retaliate against anyone who reports an incident of disability-related discrimination and/or who testifies or assists in any investigation of any violation of any provision of the ADA.

The ADA generally applies to the following employers:

- Employment agencies
- Labor unions
- Private employers with 15 or more employees
- State and local governments

According the ADA, employers are required to consider the following circumstances when determining which applicants, employees, or prospective employees qualify for protection under the ADA:

- A physical or mental impairment that could substantially limit a major physical, emotional, or mental activity such as the ability to breathe, care for oneself, hear, reason, see, talk, or walk
- Episodic impairments such as asthma or chronic obstructive pulmonary disease (COPD) or a disease like cancer that may or may not be in remission
- A history of past disabilities
- Anyone who might be treated unequally or unfairly because of a real or imagined disability

31 |

Note: For an impairment to be a legal disability, it must be long term. Temporary impairments, such as pregnancy or broken bones, are not covered by the ADA (but may be covered by other laws or regulations.)

Employers must provide reasonable accommodations

To accommodate an employee with a disability means that an employer will provide assistance and/or make appropriate changes in the job description or in the workplace to enable the employee to successfully perform his or her duties.

Accommodations might include adjusting the height of a desktop or work surface to accommodate an employee in a wheelchair or providing a distraction-free workplace for an employee with attention deficit disorder (ADD) or supplying a hearing-impaired employee with a telecommunications device for the deaf (TDD).

Negotiating accommodations with disabled employees

Employees are responsible for telling an employer about a disability and for requesting 'reasonable accommodations'. The law does not require employers to 'guess' what it will take to enable a disabled employee to successfully perform his or her job duties.

32 |

The moment an employee informs an employer of his or her disability, the employer and the employee are required by the ADA to engage in what is called a "flexible interactive process" . . . a brainstorming session during which the employee and employer work out accommodations that will make economic sense for the employer while enabling the employee to fully function in the job.

Undue hardship exception for employers

An employer does not have to provide an accommodation for a disabled employee if the accommodation would cause the employer to suffer an "undue hardship". Whether the law determines that an accommodation would be an undue hardship for an employer depends on:

- Cost of the accommodation
- The effect the accommodation would have on the organization's ability to conduct business
- The organization's structure
- The size and financial resources of the organization

Legal remedies

Legal remedies for violations of the ADA include hiring, reinstatement, promotion, back pay, front pay, restored benefits, reasonable accommodation, attorneys' fees, expert-witness fees, court costs, court ordered judgments and civil penalties.

Civil penalties for ADA violations can add up to $55,000 for a first violation or as much as $110,000 for each subsequent violation. An employer who intentionally discriminates or fails to make a 'good faith' effort to comply with ADA requirements may be court-ordered to pay additional compensatory or punitive damages.

Productivity and the Law
Louis Martin, JD
Productivity is a goal achieved only by contented employees

Chapter 10
The Fair Labor Standards Act
(FLSA) and you

THE FAIR LABOR STANDARDS ACT (FLSA) was established by Congress in 1938 to regulate minimum wage and overtime pay, to limit the number of hours in a standard workweek, to eliminate child labor abuses, and to set workforce recordkeeping standards for employers throughout America.

While the FLSA affects millions upon millions of full-time and part-time employees who work in the private and the public sectors in a wide range of jobs from cashiers to chauffeurs to clerks to nurses to physicians to teachers and on and on, some jobs are exempt or are partially exempt from some provisions of the FLSA (you can see exemptions at: http://www.dol.gov/elaws/esa/flsa/screen75.asp)

The FLSA currently requires covered nonexempt employees to be paid a minimum hourly wage of $7.25 (effective 7/24/2009). However, an employee under the age of

20 may be paid not less than $4.25 per hour during the first 90 consecutive days they are employed.

If you operate a business in which employees can receive tips, subject to other requirements, you may pay a direct hourly wage of not less than $2.13 per hour.

The first page of the Department of Labor website that describes the basics of the Fair Labor Standards Act (http://www.dol.gov/compliance/guide) takes you through more than 2,300 words of explanations, requirements, exemptions, and exceptions.

The FLSA also tells you how to compile and maintain some fairly complex employee records and tells you what types of employee rights posters, in various required languages, you must display in your workplace.

Here comes the tough part . . . the FLSA imposes some serious penalties and sanctions, including fines and 'civil money penalties' plus back pay and liquidated damages, on any employer who fails to comply with every detail of the act.

What does all of this mean to you?

It means that if the folks you trust to manage your workforce are not thoroughly trained in how to navigate the ins and outs of the FLSA, you and your organization may at some point be forced to cope with some serious, time-consuming, and costly legal and financial consequences.

Chapter 11
The Family and Medical Leave Act (FMLA) . . . keep up or else

THE FAMILY AND MEDICAL LEAVE ACT (FMLA) took effect on August 5, 1993 and allows eligible employees who work for covered employers to take up to 12 work weeks of leave in a 12-month period without pay and without risk to their jobs or loss of group health insurance coverage for the following family and medical reasons:

- The birth of a child and to care for the newborn child within one year of birth.
- To care for a child for adoption or foster care placed in the home of the employee within one year of placement.
- To care for the employee's spouse, child, or parent who has a serious health condition.

- For a serious health condition that renders the employee unable to perform the essential functions of his or her job.

- Any qualifying exigency arising from the fact that the employee's spouse, son, daughter, or parent is a covered military member on "covered active duty".

- An employee who is a covered member of the armed forces may take leave to care for a spouse, son, daughter, parent, or next of kin with a serious injury or illness for up to 26 work weeks during a single 12-month period.

A simple, even inadvertent mistake made with an employee eligible for leave under the Family and Medical Leave Act (FMLA) can drag an employer into a costly, time-consuming lawsuit.

What could possibly go wrong?

Quite a lot as it turns out.

Consider the following scenario as an illustration of what can go wrong when an employee asks for FMLA leave.

Let's say that a key employee in a busy shipping department goes to her supervisor and requests FMLA leave because her legs are hurting, the pain is getting worse, and she needs time to consult medical professionals to determine the precise treatment she needs.

Her supervisor, a dedicated employee who puts the shipping department's mission first, says, *"You gotta be kidding me! This is our busiest time of year! Why can't you put this off for another month?"*

As understandable as that supervisor's response might seem, he or she has just set up the employer for what could be considered a 'retaliation' lawsuit.

Simply stated, the FMLA allows individual employees to put personal health ahead of employer productivity.

An employer who assumes an employee's illness or injury isn't 'serious' enough to make the employee eligible for leave under the FMLA could very well be headed for a costly lawsuit.

The FMLA considers a 'serious' illness or injury to be a condition that takes 72 hours to treat with 2 or more visits with a health care professional and, by that definition, that could be a relatively simple case of flu or any number of other seemingly 'not serious' medical conditions.

While an employee injured in a car accident would be considered under the FMLA as needing to take an 'unforeseeable' leave, an employee planning to have cosmetic surgery would likely be considered under the FMLA as requesting a 'foreseeable' leave. In either case, the employer who makes the wrong FMLA determination can wind up on the wrong side of the law.

If you'd like to know more about how the FMLA defines 'foreseeable' and 'unforeseeable' leaves, go to http://www.dol.gov/whd/regs/compliance/whdfs28e.pdf for details.

When an employee returns to work after taking leave under the FMLA, he or she must be returned to the same position or to another position with the same benefits, pay, and responsibilities as came with the original position.

Any attempt to demote or replace a returning employee under the FMLA for any reason can put an employer at risk for what can be an embarrassing, costly, time-consuming legal battle.

The bottom line?

Because ignorance of the law is no excuse in any court in the land, there are two compelling reasons you should want to keep up with FMLA rules and regulations:

1. How you apply the FMLA in your organization can be complicated by the Americans with Disabilities Act (ADA), the Consolidated Omnibus Budget Reconciliation Act (COBRA), the Health Insurance

Portability and Accountability Act (HIPPA) and other laws.

2. The FMLA is a fluid law that can change overnight at the pleasure of Congress and/or the Department of Labor.

What can you do to keep up?

Go to www.dol.gov/compliance/guide/fmla for details on FMLA eligible employees and covered employers or you can call me today at 877-763-2752 or send an Email to info@hrcompliancetraining.net for a confidential, no-cost, no-obligation consultation.

Note: The FMLA applies to public agencies, including federal, local, and state employers, and local education agencies (schools) and private sector employers who employ 50 or more employees for at least 20 workweeks in the current or preceding calendar year - including joint employers and successors of covered employers.

Any employer who reveals any aspect of an employee's FMLA request or makes known any confidential medical information can be at risk for a lawsuit.

Chapter 12
How the Family and Medical Leave Act (FMLA) gave an eternal gift to a mother and daughter

WHEN BARBARA* WAS DIAGNOSED with a terminal illness and given only a few weeks to live, she desperately wanted to stay at home where she could die with dignity and in peace.

Barbara was a widow in her sixties who lived alone so she asked Sharon*, her only daughter, to care for her.

Though Sharon had a full-time career position with a long-time employer, her decision to move in with her mother for the last few weeks of her life was a choice she never questioned.

What Sharon did question was how the Family and Medical Leave Act (FMLA) would affect her decision to take an extended leave from her job.

So, Sharon met with the head of HR to ask the obvious questions:

Would her job be waiting when she returned?

And, if her job would be waiting when she returned, how would the fact that she took an extended leave affect her relationship with her employer . . . during the period of time she was off and after she returned to work?

Here's what Sharon learned.

Because Sharon had worked for at least 12 months and 1,250 hours prior to requesting leave to care for her mother and her employer had at least 50 employees, she was eligible under FMLA to take up to 12 weeks of unpaid leave during 12 months.

Sharon's employer encouraged her to use her paid sick leave first because it wouldn't count against the 12 unpaid weeks allowed under FMLA.

Sharon's employer could have asked for a certification of her mother's health condition within 5 business days but because she was a long-time, valued employee, her employer did not require any documentation.

Sharon was advised by her supervisor that a job with the same salary and benefits as she currently had would be waiting upon her return but that it might not necessarily be the same job she had before taking her leave.

Sharon took the time she needed to care for her dying mother and when she returned to work several weeks later, she readily acknowledged the fact that she would be eternally grateful for the protections afforded by the Family and Medical Leave Act.

There are several provisions and regulations that may affect an employee's decision to take leave under the FMLA and you may well want to refer employees to check out *The Employee's Guide to the Family and Medical Leave Act* by going to www.dol.gov/whd/fmla/employeeguide.pdf.

*Barbara and Sharon are pseudonyms

Chapter 13
Employee misclassification . . .
what can it cost?

WHAT IS EMPLOYEE MISCLASSIFICATION and why should you care?

You should care because if you misclassify an exempt employee as nonexempt or misclassify a nonexempt employee as exempt, you can be forced to pay back taxes plus interest and penalties.

How much?

Well, the U.S. Department of Labor (DOL) snagged more than $18 million in unpaid wages, taxes, interest, and penalties in just the past 24 months from employers who, for whatever reason, incorrectly classified employees.

There are two types of employee classifications:

1. Exempt

2. Nonexempt

And, who are exempt employees and what are they exempt from?

Exempt employees are exempt from minimum wage and overtime pay regulations in the Fair Labor Standards Act (FLSA) and typically work in administrative, executive, professional, outside sales, and in some computer and retail sales positions.

Exempt employees are not defined by job title but by job duties, must be paid a salary of at least $455.00 per week ($23,660.00 per year), and must meet other FLSA requirements . . . or not.

Employees who are nonexempt from FLSA minimum wage and overtime pay regulations typically earn less than $455.00 per week ($23,660.00 per year) and typically do not work in administrative, executive, professional, outside sales, and in some computer and retail sales positions . . . or not.

Got it?

Sounds confusing but we can work through the confusion with a quick 3-question review:

1. Would an employee who earns $20.00 an hour, works 40 hours a week, thereby earning in excess of $40,000.00 a year, be exempt from overtime regulations under FLSA that require "overtime pay for

hours worked over 40 in a workweek at a rate not less than time and one-half their regular rates of pay"?

2. Would an employee who maintains, repairs, and updates your computers, works 40 hours per week and earns $10.00 per hour ($400.00 per week), be exempt or nonexempt?

3. Would an administrative assistant who agrees to accept a $300.00 week salary to work 3 days per week be exempt or nonexempt?

Not sure?

Understandable, but as an employer, you can't afford NOT to be sure.

So, what can you do?

You can review Section 13(a) (1) of the Fair Labor Standards Act to find out about exemptions for employees who work in administrative, executive, professional, and outside sales positions.

And, you can review the Fair Labor Standards Act, 13(a) (1) and Section 13(a) (17), to understand which computer employees may or may not be exempt.

Or, you can contact the U.S. Department of Labor Wage and Hour division to ask for a copy of Fact Sheet #17A so you can study the ins and outs of regulations regarding exempt versus nonexempt employees.

And, after you've reviewed all the available relevant information you can find, you can then make an informed decision regarding each current and prospective exempt or nonexempt employee.

However, if after all that research, you still need a little more information, feel free to call me at 877-763-2752 or send an Email to info@hrcompliancetraining.net and we'll schedule a confidential, no-cost, no-obligation telephone consultation.

Caution: Because overtime pay regulations can be changed overnight by legislative action, I recommend that you regularly monitor http://www.dol.gov/whd/overtime_pay.htm

Chapter 14
How to keep up with complex employment laws and regulations

WHETHER YOU HAVE ONE OR THOUSANDS OF EMPLOYEES, you, someone else, or an entire department filled with people, can be held responsible for complying with laws and regulations that cover every aspect of Human Resources Management (HRM), including hiring, benefits management, training, labor relations, and terminations.

Employment laws and regulations issued by local, state and federal agencies may or may not apply to your particular organization, depending upon where you are located, how many people you employ, your annual revenue, and whether or not you sell products or services to governmental agencies.

Each law and regulation defines how it may or may not apply to you.

Consistency, therefore, as you might have expected, is not necessarily the name of the game when it comes to employment laws and regulations.

For example, while federal laws like the *Americans with Disabilities Act of 1990* and *Title 7 of the 1964 Civil Rights Act* apply to employers with 15 or more employees, the *Age Discrimination in Employment Act* applies to employers with 20 or more employees.

To confuse matters a bit more, the federal government's *Fair Labor and Standards Act* applies to just about every employer . . . but only if they have annual revenues of $500,000.00 or more.

Except for some nonprofits and religious organizations, California employers with 5 or more employees must comply with what is called the *Fair Employment and Housing Act* which "prohibits harassment and discrimination in employment because of race, color, religion, sex (gender), sexual orientation, marital status, national origin (including language use limitations), ancestry, mental and physical disability, medical condition (cancer/genetic characteristics), age (40 and above), pregnancy, denial of medical and family care leave, or pregnancy disability leave."

Therefore, if you're a California employer, you must comply with California's hour and wage laws and federal hour and wage laws as well.

Some counties and cities have their own minimum wage requirements while some cities, like New York City, have anti-discrimination laws in addition to state and federal anti-discrimination laws that apply to certain employers.

Dependent on your particular circumstance, you may well have to comply with all applicable employment laws and regulations . . . even when they overlap.

This means that you have to make sure that your HR policies and your employee manual reflect all applicable local, state, and federal laws and regulations.

How can you possibly keep up with every local, state, and federal employment law and regulation?

You can't.

So, what can you do?

Take heart . . . *it may not be as difficult as you might think* . . . you can go to local, state, and federal employment regulation agency websites, try to sort through all the employment laws and regulations that may apply to your organization and consult with an HR attorney to try to determine how to integrate those laws and regulations in your HR policies and employee handbook.

Or . . . you may simply attend an employment law seminar or contract with a professional to hold an employment law seminar or series of seminars at your facility.

You'll get the essential, contemporary answers you need to maintain productivity and profitability without having to take inordinate risks.

Can't ask for much more than that . . . can you?

III – DISCRIMINATION

Chapter 15
The most expensive ($160 million) employment law violation in history didn't have to happen

MERRILL LYNCH, THE VAUNTED WALL STREET brokerage firm, recently settled a racial bias suit for $160 million.

The case was filed in 2005 by African-American broker George McReynolds when only 1.3% of Merrill Lynch employees were African-American. In 25 states, Merrill Lynch hadn't hired even one African-American broker.

The McReynolds suit went beyond the numbers and alleged that because Merrill Lynch management wrongly assumed that black employees were inherently poor performers, they received minimal training and virtually no opportunities for advancement.

According to a New York Times article, Linda Friedman, McReynolds' attorney, "*told a panel of three judges that Merrill's practice of encouraging brokers to form teams* and letting departing brokers hand off customers to other team members had a disparate effect on black brokers. Black brokers were rarely invited to join teams and were too widely scattered to form their own teams. By being left out, Ms. Friedman argued, they were being left behind."

While George McReynolds was the only plaintiff when the suit was initially filed, nearly 1,200 Merrill Lynch employees eventually joined the suit as co-plaintiffs.

The legal journey was not easy or timely for the plaintiffs . . . the case languished in the federal court system for 8 years and was appealed twice to the Supreme Court.

An interesting insight to the then Merrill Lynch management racial mindset was revealed when Stanley O'Neal, Merrill Lynch's first African-American CEO (2003 to 2007) admitted that management believed that because most of their clients are white, they might not have felt comfortable entrusting their money to black brokers.

The $160 million settlement reportedly will be paid to every African-American trainee and broker employed by Merrill Lynch after May, 2001.

Epilogue: If Merrill Lynch managers had been afforded opportunities to be trained, onsite or offsite, by qualified employment law attorneys, thousands of hard-working,

55 |

dedicated African-American Merrill Lynch employees could very well have been allowed to utilize their skills, talents, and experience to help build a significantly more profitable company and Merrill Lynch could have simultaneously saved $160 million, plus legal fees, and court costs.

Employment laws in action . . . *not a bad concept, huh?*

Chapter 16
Could an age discrimination
lawsuit put you out of business?

YES . . . AN AGE DISCRIMINATION LAWSUIT COULD definitely put you out of business.

Don't believe it?

Okay then . . . *read on* . . . you just might change your mind.

Sixty-one year old Betty* was a terrific receptionist with a great smile, a magnetic personality, and an unfailing loyalty to the success of the small business where she worked with 21 co-workers.

She'd been on the job for nearly a decade, was remarkably competent, and was well-liked by colleagues, customers, and vendors.

Betty was one happy employee until the original owner decided to retire and sell the business.

The new owner didn't like Betty . . . thought she was too old.

The new owner thought that Betty sounded old on the phone and she also thought that Betty's wrinkled face and age-spotted hands made the company appear old and perhaps even feeble to anyone who entered the office.

Within days after she took over, the new owner met with the HR manager and told him to terminate Betty, saying that a receptionist with a gravelly voice, wrinkles, and age spots didn't fit the vibrant image she wanted the company to project.

The HR manager told the new owner that a long-time, competent, exceptionally loyal employee like Betty might decide to take legal action in response to being terminated without cause.

The owner said she was willing to take that chance and ordered the HR manager to terminate Betty just as soon as a younger, more attractive replacement could be found.

The HR manager reluctantly did as he was told but in the exit interview, he inadvertently revealed what the owner had said about Betty's 'crackling' voice, wrinkled face, and spotted hands.

A sorely disappointed Betty thanked the HR manager for his candor, quietly packed up her desk, left the building without comment, went home, and immediately filed a complaint with the Equal Employment Opportunity Commission (EEOC).

The EEOC sued in Federal Court on Betty's behalf and the judge hearing the case ultimately ordered the new owner to pay nearly $200,000.00 in costs and awards.

The new owner, heavily in debt to fund the purchase of the business and to pay the team of attorneys that defended her in the EEOC lawsuit, couldn't afford to pay the court-ordered judgment and was ultimately forced to shut down the business.

Could this happen to you?

It could happen to any business that discriminates against anyone because of age and, in fact, it happens quite often.

The EEOC reports that age discrimination complaints nearly doubled between 2006 and 2011.

Why?

Many experts say that when the economy slows, businesses often try to reduce labor costs by getting rid of older workers who typically earn more in wages and benefits than new, younger recruits.

While that may be the case, there is an even more ominous truth: Any business owner, manager, or HR professional who permits even one act of age discrimination clearly puts the future of the entire enterprise at risk.

The Age Discrimination in Employment Act (ADEA) prohibits any employer with 20 or more employees from discriminating on the basis of age against any employee or applicant over the age of 40. The ADEA protects an older employee's disability benefits, life insurance, pension, retirement incentives, and retirement plans.

A number of states have enacted age discrimination laws which can impact employers with fewer than 20 employees.

The best way to avoid having to pay the human and dollar costs associated with an age discrimination lawsuit is to make sure that every decision-maker . . . from the business owner to senior management to HR personnel to every key person . . . is thoroughly familiar with the ADEA and has received employment law and harassment training from a qualified, experienced employment law attorney.

*Betty is a pseudonym

IV – HARASSMENT

Chapter 17
Sexual harassment and you

SEXUAL HARASSMENT IS HUMILIATING, offensive, counterproductive, illegal, and can be quite expensive.

Consider the following press release dated 5/13/2013: *"MEMPHIS, Tenn. - A jury has rendered a verdict of more than $1.5 million in the U.S. Equal Employment Opportunity Commission's (EEOC) sexual harassment and retaliation lawsuit against New Breed Logistics, a North Carolina-based logistics services provider, the agency announced today."*

The verdict followed a seven-day trial before U.S. District Court Judge S. Thomas Anderson on behalf of four claimants and included awards of $177,094 in back pay, $486,000 in compensatory damages and $850,000 in punitive damages for the victims.

The EEOC's lawsuit charged New Breed Logistics (Chapter 46) with subjecting three female employees in Memphis to sexual harassment and retaliating against the three female employees and one male employee for opposing the harassment in violation of Title VII.

Specifically, the jury found that a New Breed warehouse supervisor harassed three temporary workers by subjecting them to unwelcome sexual touching and lewd, obscene and vulgar sexual remarks at the company's Avaya Memphis area warehouse facility.

Further, the EEOC charged and the jury agreed, a New Breed supervisor fired the three temp workers because they complained about the harassment. In addition, the EEOC said, the supervisor also retaliated against a male employee by terminating him because he opposed the harassment and agreed to serve as a witness for several claimants during the company's investigation."

EEOC definition of sexual harassment

"It is unlawful to harass a person (an applicant or employee) because of that person's sex. Harassment can include "sexual harassment" or unwelcome sexual advances, requests for sexual favors, and other verbal or physical harassment of a sexual nature.

Harassment does not have to be of a sexual nature, however, and can include offensive remarks about a person's sex. For example, it is illegal to harass a woman by making offensive comments about women in general.

63 |

Both victim and the harasser can be either a woman or a man, and the victim and harasser can be the same sex.

Although the law doesn't prohibit simple teasing, offhand comments, or isolated incidents that are not very serious, harassment is illegal when it is so frequent or severe that it creates a hostile or offensive work environment or when it results in an adverse employment decision (such as the victim being fired or demoted).

The harasser can be the victim's supervisor, a supervisor in another area, a co-worker, or someone who is not an employee of the employer, such as a client or customer."

As an employer, you are responsible for maintaining a workplace completely free of sexual harassment.

While this responsibility is clearly a legal obligation, it is also a common-sense obligation to an employer's financial stability because sexual harassment, on any level, harms morale which adversely impacts productivity, profitability, and the organization's internal and external reputations.

The first step to prevent sexual harassment in the workplace is to develop a clear, concise policy specifically designed to accommodate the unique culture of your workforce.

This policy should include a clear definition of sexual harassment, a zero-tolerance statement, a safe procedure for reporting sexual harassment complaints, an investigative procedure, a no-retaliation policy, and clear-cut disciplinary procedures.

The next step is to communicate your policy to everyone in the organization . . . *managers, supervisors, key personnel, employees, vendors, everyone* . . . to make certain there is no doubt about how your sexual harassment policy will work to protect each and every employee.

The third step is to walk your facilities . . . *to talk with employees, face-to-face, and often* . . . to make sure you take advantage of every possible opportunity to be aware of and prevent even the potential for sexual harassment.

The fourth and final step is to conduct regularly scheduled training seminars to ensure that every employee understands why and how to comply with all applicable laws and regulations regarding sexual harassment in the workplace.

Four simple, logical steps to preserve human dignity and promote productivity . . . that's all there is to sexual harassment and you.

As with anything worthwhile, there's nothing to it but to do it.

Chapter 18
How to investigate an
allegation of sexual harassment

IT'S A FRANTIC FRIDAY, the last day of the month, and you're a hands-on shipping department manager who's working hard to ship as many orders before the close of business as is humanly possible.

The company is on track to set a billing record which means bonuses for everyone in shipping and you're not about to let that opportunity slip away.

One of your best employees suddenly barges into your office, slams the door, and abruptly announces that she wants 'to talk'!

She's obviously agitated so you ask her to take a seat and you invite her to take a deep breath and speak freely about whatever is on her mind.

You've got a great crew of hard-working men and women who typically get on well together so you're taken aback when the lady angrily tells you that her boss, a well-respected, long-term packing line supervisor, has been trying to date her for months. She then claims that the supervisor just threatened to write a poor performance review if she continues to refuse to go out with him.

Though the lady is obviously upset, she tells you that she doesn't want you to discipline the line supervisor. She doesn't want to ruin the guy's reputation and put his job at risk. She only wants you to document that she reported the harassment to you . . . just in case she can't somehow ultimately convince this guy, her boss, to back off.

In an effort to make sure you completely understand the lady's accusation, you question her gently, hoping to determine what has been happening between her and the line supervisor and when, where, and why.

She answers your questions, underscores the fact that he's never touched her in any way, and describes in excruciating detail what the line supervisor has said and when and where.

And you then ask a critical question: "Has anyone witnessed him harassing you?"

Disappointment and frustration are obvious in her expression as she shakes her head and suddenly tells you that she's anxious to get back to work . . . she wants to do everything she can to help set the new billing record so she doesn't lose her bonus.

You thank the lady for her time and as she leaves, you're thinking, *not what I needed today . . . what should I do?*

Should you keep quiet for the time being and concentrate on setting that record?

After all, the line supervisor is a critical employee and, if you pull him off the job, his absence will definitely slow down shipping volume and that could kill the bonuses for lots of good employees who definitely deserve to be rewarded for their hard work and dedication.

Nevertheless, the law's the law.

I can't put a few bonuses ahead of the lady's dignity and her sense of security on the job, you think. *Shouldn't I call the line supervisor into the office, confront him, and launch an immediate investigation?*

What to do?

Investigate now . . . or not?

If you fail to investigate immediately, you'll face two serious problems.

One . . . tensions between the lady who alleged sexual harassment and the line supervisor could continue to escalate and that escalation could adversely affect the morale and productivity of other employees.

Two . . . if you don't make an immediate effort to investigate an allegation of sexual harassment, you and the organization could ultimately wind up on the wrong side of a time-consuming, reputation-killing, costly lawsuit.

So, you realize, *I really have no choice, do I?*

Like it or not, you have to do what's right, not what's fun, expedient, or financially rewarding!

In this particular scenario, you'll have to forget about the shipping record and the bonuses and immediately investigate the lady's allegation and as you do, you'll want to follow a step-by-step protocol that goes something like this:

- First things first . . . think about the relationship between the accuser and accused as you have perceived it over time. Have you seen, heard, or sensed tension between the lady and the line supervisor? If so, when, where, and why?

- And then, to confirm your perceptions, you'll have to quietly approach whomever you can trust in the department to keep your conversation confidential and ask them to describe any tensions they may have noticed between the lady and the line supervisor.

- If your perceptions and/or the perceptions of others confirm the lady's allegations and you think this may be an isolated incident, you may want to simply sit down with the line supervisor and tell him to effectively take a cold shower and immediately leave the lady alone or risk immediate termination. You document the conversation, have the line supervisor sign an acknowledgment thereof, and let the lady know what you've done . . . end of discussion.

- If, on the other hand, you have reason to believe that the lady's complaint is part of a pattern of aberrant behavior on the part of the line supervisor, you will certainly want to move forward with a more comprehensive investigation.

- In either case, as I've already said, don't sit on your hands! Despite the lady's hesitation to damage the line supervisor's reputation and put his job security at risk, you have to take *immediate action* to prevent any further incidents of harassment. Verbal harassment can unfortunately quickly devolve into more aggressive behaviors including even physical assaults and worse.

- If you do decide to move forward with a thorough investigation, get some professional help. After all, you're probably not a trained investigator or an employment law attorney and are therefore not qualified to accurately, thoroughly, and legally pursue an employment law violation investigation. Report your initial findings to HR and/or your company's legal counsel and, from that point forward, take your direction from the professionals.

- HR and counsel may determine that it is in the best interest of all concerned to suspend the line supervisor (with or without pay) pending the results of the investigation. In any case, HR and counsel will determine who to interview, when and where, and will ask a series of open-ended questions to determine the veracity and scope of the accuser's version of events.

- HR and counsel will ensure that the investigation is properly documented by recording how and when the accuser first reported the harassment, what hard evidence was revealed by the investigation, what conclusions that evidence provided, and what steps were taken . . . *before, during, and after the investigation* . . . to put an immediate end to the possibility of future harassment.

- If the line supervisor is not terminated, HR and counsel and (in this case) you will follow up not only with the accuser but with the accused and others to confirm that the harassment will never again occur.

- Additionally, you and your organization will definitely want to determine systemic causes, if any, behind this situation. Systemic causes can include employee confusion about your organization's HR policies and procedures, the failure to schedule training sessions to help senior management, key personnel, supervisors, and all other employees stay current on applicable local, state, and federal employment laws and regulations, and/or other combinations of organizational failures to protect and preserve the dignity of all employees.

Epilogue: There are no surprises here . . . sexual harassment, like any form of harassment in the workplace is not only illegal and completely unnecessary, it assaults the dignity of men and women, destroys morale, damages personal and professional reputations, and kills productivity and is therefore totally unacceptable in any workplace, under any circumstance.

Chapter 19
Workplace harassment and you

WORKPLACE HARASSMENT . . . *morale destroyer, productivity killer, profit eater, reputation slayer* . . . whatever you call it, workplace harassment is neither legal nor necessary.

As an employer, you know that workplace harassment is a violation of Title VII of the Civil Rights Act of 1964 and can be a violation of the Age Discrimination in Employment Act of 1967, and/or the Americans with Disabilities Act of 1990.

You also know that federal law can hold individuals as well as organizations liable for potential costs, judgments, and penalties associated with any act of harassment by any employee, key person, manager, owner, or supervisor in the workplace.

Acts of workplace harassment can be committed not just by employees, managers and supervisors but by vendors and others in and around the workplace and is defined by the U.S. Equal Employment Opportunity Commission (EEOC) as follows:

"Harassment is unwelcome conduct that is based on race, color, religion, sex (including pregnancy), national origin, age (40 or older), disability or genetic information. Harassment becomes unlawful where 1) enduring the offensive conduct becomes a condition of continued employment, or 2) the conduct is severe or pervasive enough to create a work environment that a reasonable person would consider intimidating, hostile, or abusive. Anti-discrimination laws also prohibit harassment against individuals in retaliation for filing a discrimination charge, testifying, or participating in any way in an investigation, proceeding, or lawsuit under these laws; or opposing employment practices that they reasonably believe discriminate against individuals, in violation of these laws.

Petty slights, annoyances, and isolated incidents (unless extremely serious) will not rise to the level of illegality. To be unlawful, the conduct must create a work environment that would be intimidating, hostile, or offensive to reasonable people."

The best way to avoid liability under applicable anti-harassment laws is to: 1. Proactively take whatever steps are necessary to be aware of and to prevent even the potential for workplace harassment and, 2. To promptly put an end to any incident of harassing behavior and, 3. To be able to prove, if necessary, that a harassed employee failed, without cause, to take advantage of your efforts to prevent or correct any incident of harassment.

The most certain way for you to eliminate harassment in the workplace is to clearly and concisely communicate zero-tolerance anti-harassment policies to all employees and to provide consistent, quality interactive anti-harassment employment law training.

Chapter 20
An example of workplace harassment unchecked (based on an actual event)

THE OWNER OF A MANUFACTURING COMPANY in a small southwestern town had a penchant for harassing his employees with rants and raves whenever things didn't go his way.

It was 2008, the Great Recession was raging, and good-paying full-time jobs with benefits were virtually nonexistent.

In light of that unfortunate fact, the company owner realized that he could get away with his harassing rants by threatening to fire anyone who might even think about filing a complaint with any agency under any circumstance.

And . . . so, on a hot Friday afternoon, the red-faced owner stormed into his HR manager's office, waving an official looking letter and, scowling with rage, screamed, "This letter from the Department of Labor says that you admitted to a DOL auditor that we knowingly misclassified sales people? What were you thinking? Have you lost your mind?"

The HR manager stood behind her desk and calmly said, "Please do not shout at me. You misclassified those employees behind my back to reduce payroll taxes, something I never knew until the DOL audit. You wouldn't expect me to lie to a government auditor, would you?"

"Have you any idea," the owner shouted, "how much your stupidity is going to cost me?"

"I'll ask you again," the HR manager said calmly, "to not shout at me."

"Shut your mouth," he spat, raising his right hand as he moved toward her, "before I shut it for you!"

The HR manager reached for the phone on her desk, pressed 9-1-1, waited for the operator to come on the line, identified herself, gave her location, and said, "My employer has just threatened to physically harm me and I would like you to send a pol . . ."

The owner's lips were a thin line of pure rage as he grabbed the receiver from the HR manager's hand, smashed the phone to the floor, and slapped her across the face. "No one calls the cops on me," he hissed.

Resisting the urge to slap back, the HR manager pressed her arms to her sides with so much effort that her shoulders burned with pain.

Without another word, the business owner stormed out of the HR manager's office.

The lady took a moment to compose herself, grabbed her purse from the credenza behind her desk, and walked out to the parking lot to wait for police to arrive*.

Unchecked workplace harassment often escalates to workplace violence; a serious social and economic problem with wide-ranging consequences for all concerned.

According to the Department of Labor, approximately two million people throughout the U.S. every year are victims of various forms of workplace violence.

No matter what form it takes, workplace harassment and/or violence, is completely unacceptable because it not only hurts people physically and emotionally but also kills morale, destroys productivity, and costs billions of dollars in lost productivity each year.

Workplace harassment and violence awareness and prevention begins and ends with educated, thinking men and women . . . *business owners, executives, HR managers, key personnel, supervisors, and team leaders* . . . who care enough to invest time and money in learning how to develop, communicate, and implement manageable HR policies to eliminate the potential for workplace harassment and violence in any form.

The business owner was jailed for assault, closed his business, and ultimately settled a civil suit with the HR manager for an undisclosed amount.

V – MANAGING AND THE LAW

Chapter 21
How to construct HR policies to protect employees, profits, and personal and professional reputations

ANY ORGANIZATION THAT CONSTRUCTS AN HR POLICY at the wrong time, in the wrong place, for the wrong reasons will undoubtedly implement a policy that ultimately fails to protect its employees, profits, and image.

I'm talking about the HR policy that is typically created immediately after management realizes that the organization is not compliant with one or more employment laws and is therefore vulnerable to costly lawsuits, huge settlements, bad publicity, and drops in employee morale.

It happens like this: Senior managers suddenly discover that the organization is not 'HR Compliant'. Managers then scramble to cobble together a new HR policy to eliminate the immediate problem based on what they think will work, based on what they've heard other companies do, and perhaps even based on perfunctory internet searches. They then string together enough words to create a policy that at least seems to make sense, issue the obligatory in-house announcement, and breathe easier as they walk away, thinking that the new policy will protect the organization.

Odds are, unfortunately, those managers very likely won't breathe easy for long.

Why?

Because they failed to follow the following logical steps:

- The first step is to consider how your new HR policy may or may not interact with local and state employment laws (like state-specific Family Medical Leave laws) and how that interaction or lack thereof might affect your new HR policy.

- The second step is to make sure that you clearly understand how your new HR policy will work with . . . or against . . . federal laws like the Americans with Disabilities Act of 1990 (ADA), the Age Discrimination in Employment Act of 1967 (ADEA), family leave and wage-hour laws, and others.

- The third step is consult with an employment law attorney to help you write your new HR policy as a policy, not as a legal contract that could adversely impact your case in a potential employment lawsuit.

- The fourth step is to consistently train supervisors, key personnel, and employees in how to integrate the new policy with other policies in your HR manual. New employees and newly promoted or recently hired supervisors should of course be trained on all HR policies as soon after their hire date or date of promotion as is possible.

I hope that this chapter will be useful in helping you implement HR policies that work to protect your employees, your profits, and your personal and professional reputations.

Chapter 22
What is an HR audit
and why should you care?

WHAT IS AN HR AUDIT?

An HR Audit is an objective in-house review you should frequently conduct to compare and contrast your theoretical and real HR policies, practices, and procedures with the essential employment laws (see Chapter 6, page 20).

You should care about an HR audit because it can eliminate your risk of inadvertently (or otherwise) committing employment law violations that can not only destroy productivity but can also result in attorney fees, court costs, judgments, and fines assessed against your organization and/or individual directors, executives, key personnel, managers, and supervisors.

Regularly scheduled HR audits can help guarantee that your organization remains consistently compliant with local, state, and federal laws and regulations by maintaining a respectful, safe, productive, and profitable work environment for each and every employee.

HR audits evaluate how your organization manages the employment life cycle from recruiting new employees to hiring, to benefit enrollment, to protecting confidential information, to training, to how you manage paid and unpaid employee leave, to promotions, to an employee's exit from your organization by layoff, resignation, retirement, or termination.

HR audits also measure the effectiveness of your current HR policies, practices, and procedures by assessing the causes and effects of employee absenteeism, complaints, lawsuits, overall satisfaction or lack thereof, and turnover.

A comprehensive HR audit includes a thorough review of your organization's current HR policies, practices, and procedures and will help prepare key personnel, managers, and supervisors to:

- Recruit, interview, select, and onboard the right candidate for the right job . . . every time, all the time.
- Understand, be aware of, monitor, and prevent workplace harassment in all forms.
- Develop the skills they need to effectively coach and counsel employees.

- Effectively and legally document employee behaviors.
- Apply the strategies and tactics required to create a safe, productive workplace environment.
- Promote workplace ethics.
- Prevent bias, discrimination and prejudice in the workplace.
- Effectively manage a diverse workforce.
- Properly apply provisions of the Americans With Disabilities Act (ADA).
- Properly apply provisions of the Fair Labor Standards Act (FLSA).
- Properly apply provisions of the Family Medical Leave Act (FMLA).

When you've completed your HR audit, you will want to objectively analyze the results and implement appropriate changes in policies, practices, and procedures to ensure that you are 100% compliant with all local, state, and federal employment laws and regulations.

Chapter 23
Department of Labor (DOL) investigators are on the way . . . what now?

YOU STROLL INTO THE YOUR FIRM'S LOBBY on a bright Monday morning, happy as happy can be, looking forward to another productive day.

You are the general manager of a busy, profitable distribution company with nearly 200 employees working in a single location.

You chirp good morning to your receptionist, smile at a couple of employees hanging around the coffee maker, and suddenly notice your secretary approaching at a fast clip.

Her face is ashen and she looks distraught.

She motions you into your office, closes the door, and tremulously tells you that she just received a call from a local U.S. Department of Labor (DOL) office to say that investigators are on their way and should arrive at any minute.

As you drop into the chair behind your desk, you ask your secretary why the DOL is sending investigators but all she can do is frown and say she hasn't got a clue.

You're perplexed, wondering whether one of your employees might have filed a complaint with the DOL but you can't imagine why. There have been no recent disciplinary actions and employees, to a man and a woman, are treated well at your company, turnover rates are low, and pay is at or above average for similar jobs in the area.

You dial your chief accountant's extension and ask the critical question: "Why on earth would the Department of Labor want to investigate us and why would they make a surprise visit?"

Your chief accountant says that DOL could be on the way to investigate a complaint by a current or former employee or it could just be a random audit . . . though, she quickly adds, while it is unusual for the DOL to conduct a surprise investigation or audit, it is not unheard of.

She also says that DOL investigators may be looking for evidence to prove that the firm has somehow violated the Fair Labor Standards Act (FLSA). That means, she says, DOL investigators will want to review original payroll records and may even want to walk the facility to physically count employees to match employment records with live bodies.

You thank her, hang up, and hustle down to the payroll department, enter the payroll manager's office, close the door behind you, tell her what's up, and ask her to confirm that payroll time and attendance records are accurate and up to date.

She raises an apprehensive eyebrow and assures you that although she's certain there is no cause for concern, she'll review the records ... straightaway.

As you hurry back to your office to wait for the DOL investigators to show up, you can't help but think about the obvious questions.

Should I call the DOL, you wonder, *to ask what they want?* But you immediately answer your own question . . . *No.* DOL investigators are in the business of finding, correcting, and punishing mistakes, not warning employers in advance.

And then you wonder, *which current or former employee could have filed a complaint and why?* But you immediately realize that even if someone did file a complaint, it doesn't matter who complained or why . . . what's done is done.

Then you wonder, *should I designate a team like, our chief accountant, our payroll manager, and our HR manager, to meet with DOL investigators or should I try to handle this myself?* You realize that there is strength in numbers and, if investigators do find something wrong, you know that your team is likely to come up with better solutions than you'd come up with on your own.

You conclude that the best thing you can do is to view the DOL investigation as an opportunity to improve how the firm records, tracks, and documents employee time and attendance and processes payrolls.

While you wait, you sketch out the following five point plan to handle this investigation:

1. You'll assign one key person to head the team that will work with the Department of Labor . . . that will streamline communications and speed up the process.

2. You'll request a pre-audit meeting between yourself, your key person, and DOL investigators to talk about how you can best to help them achieve their goals.

3. For all the right reasons, you'll assign one person to review every document before you release a copy to investigators.

4. Your team will fully document every DOL request for employee information, payroll and benefits data and history, and any other records requested.

Productivity and the Law
Louis Martin, JD
Productivity is a goal achieved only by contented employees

5.   Everyone in your firm will fully cooperate with DOL investigators, will be 100% honest, and will treat investigators with dignity and respect.

As you finish laying out your plan, you begin to think about how you and your team can make sure the firm is fully prepared for future DOL investigations . . . surprise or not . . . and, as the receptionist calls to advise that the investigators have arrived, you wonder, *why on earth weren't we prepared for this before today?*

Chapter 24
Employment "at-will" . . .
what does it mean?

IN MOST STATES, *EMPLOYMENT "AT-WILL"* means that an employer can legally terminate an employee at any time for any reason or for no reason without liability.

At the same time, "at-will" employees can leave an employer's organization at any time for any reason or for no reason at all without liability.

If, however, an employer offers a verbal or written contract to an applicant or employee, the terms and conditions of that contract will determine when, why, and how that applicant can be rejected or that employee can be terminated.

Fairly straightforward . . . *right?*

Right . . . except for the following exceptions:

The 'discrimination' exception . . . it is against the law in most states and it is against federal law for any employer to discriminate against an employee, *any employee,* because of age, color, disability, gender, national origin, race, religion, or sexual orientation. The termination of an employee for any of those 'reasons' would presumably not be protected by the "at-will" concept under the law.

According to the *Center for American Progress*, lawsuits filed on behalf of applicants and employees claiming some form of discrimination cost American businesses nearly $70 billion in legal costs and court-ordered awards in 2012.

Applicant and employee discrimination occurs in the hallowed halls of some of the biggest names in corporate America.

FEDEX, for example, arguably one of the best-known corporations in the world, was ordered by the Department of Labor in 2012 to pay $3 million to settle discrimination claims by job applicants in more than a dozen states.

There can be a "just cause" promise exception . . . if an employer advises an employee, verbally and/or in writing, that he or she will not be terminated without "just cause" or if an employer defines terms under which he or she may be terminated, a court may well determine that that employee is protected by an 'implied' employment contract and is therefore not employed 'at-will'.

There is also a 'public policy' exception . . . an employer may not terminate an employee if that termination violates public policy. For example, an employer cannot fire an employee for reporting discrimination, harassment, illegal activities, and safety violations and cannot terminate an employee who exercises his or her legal rights like taking family leave, jury-duty leave, medical leave, or military leave.

Epilogue . . . Employers must remember that "at-will" exceptions apply to even problem employees; exceptions which can complicate an employer's perceived need to terminate an employee whose attitudes and behaviors may in any way negatively impact morale and productivity.

Additionally, employers cannot ignore the fact that in the information age, employees are keenly aware of their rights under state and federal laws and are therefore more likely than ever to pursue legal action whenever they think that they've been wrongfully terminated.

The bottom line?

Employer beware . . . make sure that each employee understands his or her "at-will" status or lack thereof.

Chapter 25
Constructive discharge . . .
what does it really mean?

A CONSTRUCTIVE DISCHARGE SOUNDS LIKE an employer "constructively discharges" (terminates) an employee in the best interests of all concerned.

Right?

Wrong.

A "constructive discharge" occurs when an employer forces an employee to resign or retire by creating or allowing a hostile or intolerable work environment in which that employee is forced to attempt to do his or her job.

Intolerable working conditions include situations in which the employee is subjected to discrimination and/or harassment, a demotion, arbitrary cuts in benefits and pay and/or overwhelming increases in workload.

Courts have held that a constructive discharge can be caused by the purposeful or inadvertent behaviors of coworkers, key personnel, managers, supervisors, and/or senior management, or by official or unofficial employer policies.

The following factors may be considered by a court of competent jurisdiction when an employee files a "constructive discharge" lawsuit:

- Behaviors intended to intimidate, isolate, manipulate, or involve any form of sexual abuse.
- Demotion.
- Destructive behaviors under the color of authority.
- Elimination of job duties.
- Involuntary transfer to a less desirable position.
- Physical assault or threat of physical assault.
- Reassignment to a menial or degrading job.
- Salary reduction.
- Threat of termination.
- Verbal or physical harassment or humiliation by coworkers, key personnel, supervisors, and senior management.

Though some state and federal courts have been ambivalent in their rulings on constructive discharge cases, the Equal Employment Opportunity Commission (EEOC) is not at all ambivalent. The EEOC considers constructive discharge to be a discriminatory practice, a chargeable offense for which an organization and even individuals can be sued and ultimately fined and/or ordered to pay cash settlements to 'constructively discharged' employees.

Most employment law attorneys agree that the losses in productivity that can result from even one constructive discharge can be even more costly in the final analysis than resultant legal fees, court costs, fines, and court-ordered judgments.

How can you avoid finding yourself and your organization trapped in a 'constructive discharge' case?

At the risk of sounding like I'm over simplifying, training is the answer.

This isn't theory . . . it's fact.

The proof is what it is . . . employers who invest in training employees, key personnel, managers, supervisors, and senior managers in proven strategies and tactics to watch for and prevent a hostile, unbearable workplace, are simply not likely to find themselves on the wrong end of a "constructive discharge" lawsuit.

Chapter 26
Progressive employee discipline; your best insurance policy?

PROGRESSIVE EMPLOYEE DISCIPLINE is a graduated series of employer approaches, from *easy* (an informal verbal or written reprimand) to *tough* (suspension or termination), to manage employee behavior or performance.

Whether they call it corrective action procedures, performance improvement, positive discipline, or something else, most employers recognize the value of utilizing some form of progressive employee discipline.

Progressive discipline provides a number of benefits for employers and employees, including but not limited to:

- Improved communication between key personnel, managers, supervisors, and employees.
- Improvements in employee morale and reduced turnover by virtue of consequences for poor performance and rewards for good performance.

98 |

Productivity and the Law
Louis Martin, JD
Productivity is a goal achieved only by contented employees

- Supervisors are able to intervene and take steps to correct negative behaviors at the first sign of trouble.
- Supervisors are able to coach, train, and motivate troubled employees to become productive, valued assets.

If you ever find yourself on the wrong side of a wrongful termination lawsuit, you may be surprised to discover that there are no laws that require employers to implement a progressive discipline policy.

Nevertheless, if you ever do wind up defending yourself against a wrongful termination lawsuit and you don't have or don't use a progressive employee discipline policy, the court you face will very likely decide against you, exposing you to fines, judgments, court costs, and perhaps even a big hit to your reputation.

Simply stated, courts expect employers to play fair with employees and, from the court's perspective, fair in wrongful terminations cases is often defined by the employer's progressive discipline policy or lack thereof.

It would be nice if employees arrived each day ready, willing, and able to perform to the best of their abilities but employees are people and people sometimes show up late, miss deadlines, don't always get along, often fail to perform, and don't always put safety first.

An employer, therefore, must be able to rely on a viable, legally defensible progressive employee discipline policy to motivate and enable employees to create and sustain a productive workplace.

A progressive employee discipline policy typically works like this:

1. **Verbal warning** – A supervisor invites an employee to meet behind closed doors to discuss the employer's concern. The supervisor clearly states the problem and asks for and carefully listens to the employee's response. The supervisor then asks the employee to help develop an action plan with a timeline to correct the problem. The conversation and the corrective action plan are documented, acknowledged by the employee, and placed in the employee's permanent file.

2. **First written warning** – If the employee fails to keep his or her commitment to the action plan or other problems arise, the supervisor documents the employer's concerns, clarifies the required behavioral, performance, or safety standards, and provides a

timeline for improvement. The supervisor informs the employee that continued failures to perform may result in termination. The written warning is acknowledged by the employee and placed in the employee's permanent file.

3. **Final written warning** – If the employee continues to fail to meet the employer's behavioral, performance, or safety standards, the supervisor gives the employee a final written warning along with a copy of the first written warning, lays out the actions the employee must take, and provides a corresponding action timeline. The final written warning is acknowledged by the employee and placed in the employee's permanent file.

4. **Pre-termination review** – If the employee continues to fail to meet the employer's standards, the supervisor asks key personnel, senior management, or the human resources department to review the employee's situation. The employee is confronted with prior warning documentation and is given the opportunity to respond. Dependent on circumstances, it may be necessary at this point in the progressive employee discipline process to suspend

the employee, with or without pay, until the review is completed.

5. **Termination** – If there are no open employer-employee contractual issues and/or if there is no reason to believe that termination at this point could appear to be an act of retaliation on any level, the written decision to terminate is provided to the employee and the termination takes effect.

Epilogue - Progressive employee discipline is designed not to help employers justify employee terminations but to improve employee behaviors, performance, and productivity.

For that reason, we recommend that you consult an employment law professional who can help you tailor the progressive employee discipline plan that will work best for your employees and your organization.

When you consider the billions of dollars in fines, judgments, and legal costs incurred by U.S. employers every year, your progressive discipline policy could be your best business insurance policy.

Chapter 27
You, employee performance logs, and the law

HAS THIS EVER HAPPENED TO YOU?

It's that dreaded time of the year again . . . you know what we mean, don't you?

Employee evaluation time!

There's no way out so you block out some quiet time, close the office door, and turn off your phones and Email alarms, grit your teeth, and get to work.

You snatch the first employee file off the stack, open it, scan the name and sigh, shaking your head.

What the heck?

It's happened again.

You're supposed to be evaluating this individual's performance for the past year but you can't remember more than a few weeks back and while what you do remember wasn't all that bad, it wasn't all that good either.

Hmmm.

What to do, what to do?

If you give the employee a poor review because you can't really remember the good, you risk hurting her future with the company . . . you might even set yourself and the company up to be sued by a justifiably angry employee.

If, on the other hand, you give the employee a good review because you can't remember the bad, you risk setting her up for a future promotion she might not be able to handle.

Hmmm.

The point is, it is risky to try to rely solely on memory to log, evaluate, and document employee performance . . . especially when you're doing it after the fact.

The better approach is to create an employment performance log for each employee and to then keep it up . . . consistently . . . daily, weekly, whatever.

By the way, an employment performance log does not have to be complicated. You can easily keep track of employee performance on sheets of lined notebook paper you can stick in a 3-ring binder or in a personnel file in a locked drawer or you can keep employee performance logs in encrypted files on your computer.

No matter what form your employment performance logs may take, it is important for all the right reasons to document employee performance accurately, thoroughly, and consistently.

How?

The following tips can help make your life easier . . . a lot easier when employee evaluation time comes:

- **Play fair with every employee by recording the good and the bad . . . as it happens.** The sooner you record an entry, for better or for worse, in an employee's file, the more accurate and timely your performance evaluation will ultimately be.

- **Note the day, date, and time of each entry as if you are preparing evidence for a court because that may well be exactly what you're doing.** Remember . . . any performance evaluation can be challenged by any employee in any court, under any circumstance, so make sure your evaluation is complete, objective, and, most important, accurate.

- **Write your observations as if the whole world, including your boss, your parents, and perhaps even your high school sweetheart, will read them.** Include the good with the bad and be honest and objective about each behavior you observe. Do not, under any circumstance, include gossip or make any assumptions about an employee's motives or try to psychoanalyze him or her in any way. Make sure you never allow a personal bias to cause you to get snarky in an employment performance log, especially when you're writing about an employee's age, disability, gender, marital status, race or religious or sexual orientation.

- **Be concise but thorough by giving specific examples of positive and negative on-the-job behaviors.** If Joe does not work well with others in the department he supervises, don't say, "Joe does not work well with others", say, "Joe has refused to take advantage of a supervisory training class the company has offered." Or, instead of saying, "Shirley is a good, reliable, employee," say something more informative like, "Shirley's leadership skills helped to improve productivity by 25% in the last quarter."

In summary, as a key person, manager, or supervisor, you are responsible for objectively, fairly, and legally logging, evaluating, and reporting employee on-the-job performance.

Don't do it right and you risk harming employee morale (and productivity) and you risk putting yourself and your organization on the wrong side of potentially costly, time-consuming, reputation-killing lawsuits.

So . . . for the right reasons, do it right!

You'll be forever glad you did.

Chapter 28
HR recruiting
and interviewing checklist

THE GREATEST CHALLENGE HR PROFESSIONALS face today is hiring the right candidate for the right job for the right reasons . . . without violating employment laws.

With local, state, and federal regulators constantly looking over your shoulders these days, you'd be well advised to have a simple, straightforward recruiting and interviewing checklist you can use to prevent your organization from committing costly, potentially morale killing employment law violations . . . a checklist that would help you:

- Double-check each job posting to make sure there are no preferences that might violate local, state, or federal employment laws or regulations and ensure that each recruiting effort reaches out to a diverse cross-section of candidates.

- Review job application forms and job descriptions to ensure compliance with the Americans with Disabilities Act (ADA) and other applicable local, state, and federal employment laws. Your application forms are the first impression your organization makes on a prospective employee and they should be easy to navigate and should ask only legal, job-related questions. Don't forget to include caveats about penalties for falsifying responses and a statement on your policy on "at-will employment".

- Review job applicant interviewing protocols to make sure that every interviewee is asked the same job-related questions. You will want to tell interviewers to never ask an interviewee about age, arrest record, disability, marital status, or sexual orientation or any other life-circumstance that might violate any employment law or regulation.

The top 10 essential interview questions – Let's face it; the point of the interview is for the employer to have an opportunity to know whether it should risk making an investment in an applicant . . . the following 'essential' questions are designed to help any interviewer to make an informed decision before risking that investment.

1. The first essential question you'll want to ask is the quintessential question, the question that can set the tone for the entire interview: **"What are your minimum salary requirements?"** If the applicant's expectations and the position's salary don't match, the applicant won't be happy and will likely fail the interview, making further questions quite possibly unnecessary.

2. **"Why did you apply with us for this particular position?"** It's an open-ended, fair question, the answer to which can give you a useful insight into the character and motives of the applicant.

3. **"Why should we hire you?"** A candidate who knows her skills, talents, and goals and has researched your firm will be able to give an easy, honest answer. If the applicant can't answer this question to your satisfaction, you may well want to consider moving on to the next applicant.

4. **"What was your favorite job and why?"** The applicant's answer to this question will give you an insight into the applicant's true interests, motives, and commitment to work.

5. **"What was your least favorite job and why?"** The answer to this question can help fill in any gaps in the applicant's answer to question 3.

6. If the candidate is currently employed, you will want to ask, **"Why are you leaving your current job?"** If the candidate is currently unemployed, you will want to ask, **"Why did you leave your last job?"** This is a 'check-question', a question that will help you 'check' answers to related questions to help you spot any potential red flags regarding the applicant's job expectations and/or work ethic.

7. **"Tell me about your greatest professional success and your worst professional failure?"** The answer to this question will give you a unique insight into how the applicant creates success and how she handles failure; two critical character traits you will want to be aware of and understand in any serious candidate.

8. **"Where do you see yourself 5 years from now?"** The applicant's answer will tell you how or if the applicant believes that the job she's interviewing for today will or will not fit in with her overall future career plan.

9. **"How do you like to be managed?"** The answer to this question will help you determine how well the

applicant will fit into your organization's particular culture and management style.

10. **"Do you have any questions for me?"** Most applicants assume that the interviewer who asks this seemingly benign question is simply being polite when in fact the interviewer is 'capping' the interview to determine how much time and energy . . . *if any* . . . the applicant has invested in researching the organization and the position for which she has applied. If the applicant answers with any form of "No" to this question, you may want to think about moving on to another candidate.

Epilogue: The interview is the essential part of the recruiting process because a face-to-face dialogue creates your best opportunity to look beyond whatever you may have learned about an applicant in the application, the resume, the background check, and in references, any or all of which can, *inadvertently or otherwise,* be ambiguous.

Your job as an interviewer is to understand to the best of your ability the potential for the applicant to be a good potential investment . . . *or not* . . . and the essential questions will help you make the right decision for the right reasons.

How essential is that?

Chapter 29
On-site employment law training . . . yes, no, maybe?

WHICH IS BETTER . . . an on-site employment law training seminar provided by an outside professional organization or an in-house employment law workshop provided by someone in your human resources department?

In other words, should you invite an outside professional to train your organization on employment law complexities or can you rely on in-house HR staff to train employees to ensure your organization's ability to remain consistently compliant with various local, state, and federal employment laws?

Whether you have a fully-staffed HR department or one person handles your organization's HR responsibilities, is it reasonable to assume that your staff of one or more is capable of making sure that every manager, every supervisor, and every other employee understands and can correctly apply each and every local, state, and federal employment law and regulation to every situation in your workplace?

Your answer, hopefully, is yes . . . because an even inadvertent violation of just one of the myriad of employment laws and regulations that can apply to your organization may well put you in front of a judge, facing legal costs and fees plus individual and/or organizational fines and damages . . . with potentially huge dents in employee morale along with hits to organizational or even personal reputations.

The risk here comes from the fact that you are obligated by law to make sure that each and every HR professional, manager, supervisor, and every other employee in your organization has current, thorough working knowledge of every applicable local, state, and federal employment law and regulation.

So . . . the critical question is, which is the best way . . . *on-site or in-house* . . . to provide training to protect your organization, you, and your employees from the potential liabilities that come with violations of employment laws and regulations you may not even know?

Which is the better choice?

Most private and public organizations have concluded that in-house employment law training can, over time, become burdensome, complicated, inefficient, and extremely expensive for two reasons: 1. In-house trainers typically have other responsibilities and find it difficult to keep up with ever-changing local, state, and federal employment laws and regulations and, 2. Even the most effective HR manager and staffer is not necessarily trained, experienced, or motivated to be an effective teacher.

Onsite employment law seminars can often be the better choice for two compelling reasons:

1. A full-time employment law professional, usually an employment law attorney, consistently stays current on local, state, and federal employment laws and regulations.

2. Employment law seminar facilitators are experienced, skilled, talented, thoroughly trained teachers fully capable of communicating facts, figures, and the subtleties of every aspect of employment laws and regulations.

If you would like to know more about how . . . or whether . . . you can benefit from on-site employment law training, please call 877-763-2752 or send an Email to info@hrcompliancetraining.net for a confidential, no-cost, no-obligation consultation.

Chapter 30
How to choose the right
HR compliance trainer

THERE IS NO DOUBT ABOUT IT . . . HR compliance can be a risky proposition; a proposition that has the potential to kill an entire organization. How an organization cares for its workforce, after all, can be the single most critical factor to its success, yet HR compliance is an all-too often neglected in the day-to-day operations of most organizations.

You know how it goes . . . in the hustle and bustle of daily activities required to deliver first-rate, value-added products and services to your customers, you don't always have the time it takes to make sure your organization is compliant with every single applicable local, state, and federal HR laws and regulation.

Nevertheless, because you're keenly aware of the risks . . . *unhappy employees, lost productivity, and potential legal liabilities* . . . faced by any non-compliant organization, you want to do what is right for all concerned.

116 |

You know that it makes people sense and economic sense to be 100% HR compliant.

You realize that HR compliance involves defining, communicating, and maintaining a complex set of policies that define behaviors of all employees; behaviors that must comply with a variety of laws and regulations enforced by various governing agencies.

You know how critical it is for you to integrate HR compliance into your organization's operational strategies and tactics . . . while keeping up with the latest changes to HR regulations and laws.

At the same time, you aren't sure that a one-size-fits-all solution like a CD presentation or a webinar is the best path to HR compliance in your organization.

And, you're right.

The best way to make sure that your organization remains HR compliant is to seek out the expertise you can get only from an experienced employment law attorney.

An employment law attorney can provide sensible, workable solutions to every aspect of HR compliance, solutions that will work for you not only because they are based upon current regulations and laws but because they meet the unique needs of your workplace culture.

Chapter 31
How to generate a return on your investment in employment law compliance training

RETURN ON INVESTMENT (ROI) determines the long-term viability of your business.

While your organization works hard to generate reasonable ROI from every product and service it sells, if you fail to protect profits from the legal fees, court costs, fines, and judgments that can result from employment law violations, you might as well forget about long-term viability.

Dependent upon how, when, and why you invest in training your workforce about the ins and outs of employment law, your return on that investment can be as significant as the sum total of losses you prevent . . . losses that can potentially add up to thousands, hundreds of thousands, or even millions of dollars.

According to the Department of Labor (DOL) and the Equal Employment Opportunity Commission (EEOC), nearly 70% of all employers in America fail to comply with one or more employment laws or regulations.

For that reason, employers pay nearly a quarter of a billion dollars each year in fines and penalties, plus legal fees and court costs . . . costs drawn directly from the bottom line of every organization that finds itself on the wrong side of an employment law violation.

Labor lawyers report that the typical jury award for damages for an employment law violation averages $600,000.00, plus court-ordered fines and legal costs.

In many employment law cases, losses become particularly personal and painful when courts order company owners, officers, and key personnel to pay huge personal fines and/or even serve time behind bars.

An unforgettable example of this painful outcome was the president of a Midwest company who was found guilty of violating the Fair Labor Standards Act (FLSA) and was ordered to pay a fine in excess of $3 million and sentenced to serve two years in prison.

The DOL and the EEOC do not hesitate to investigate, charge, and prosecute even some of the biggest names in American business . . . *Bank of America, Home Depot, United*

Parcel Service, and dozens of other Fortune 500 corporations that have lost hundreds of millions of dollars in profits simply because they failed to adequately invest in employment law compliance training.

In addition to the huge savings and precious peace of mind that effective employment law compliance training brings to business owners, officers, and managers, a workforce thoroughly trained in the latest employment laws and regulations will undoubtedly be a more productive and therefore more profitable workforce.

Isn't that the point?

Chapter 32
The best HR compliance policy is common sense (but you already knew that, didn't you?)

HR COMPLIANCE DOES NOT HAVE TO BE complicated . . . not really.

HR compliance is, after all, more common sense than anything else.

Think about it . . . who could possibly disagree with the following simple premise? The employer who is sensible enough to implement common sense HR compliance policies to create a respectful, safe work environment is much less likely to wind up on the wrong side of the law.

If you work with your employees to proactively prevent workforce conflict, you not only demonstrate your commitment to complying with local, state, and federal employment laws and regulations, you demonstrate your respect and concern for employees . . . by far the best way to boost morale and productivity.

The best HR compliance policy incorporates the following common sense elements:

- Regularly scheduled audits to make sure that HR policies and documentation comply with current laws and regulations.
- A regularly updated employee handbook to educate employees on organizational expectations and legal requirements for workplace behaviors and activities.
- Accurate, current job descriptions to clearly define each position in the organization and help senior management monitor productivity relative to each job description.
- Consistent, timely performance appraisals to help employees who fall behind in productivity to improve and to recognize and motivate employees who excel on the job.
- A practical, transparent action plan to proactively prevent various forms of workplace discrimination.
- Regularly scheduled employment law seminars to provide employees and key personnel with meaningful opportunities to learn how to prevent

costly, time-consuming violations of local, state, and federal employment laws and regulations.

How can you get started on developing a common sense HR compliance policy?

Simple . . . you can call me today at 877-763-2752 or send an Email to info@hrcompliancetraining.net for a confidential, no-cost, no-obligation consultation.

Chapter 33
Keep up to keep yourself and your organization out of court

YOU'RE A HARD-WORKING HR PROFESSIONAL coping with employment laws and regulations that can change as frequently and as abruptly as the political winds that blow in and out of county seats, state capitols, and in Washington, D.C.

You're charged with the awesome responsibility of making sure that your organization never steps outside the boundaries set by politicians who created comprehensive legislation like the Americans with Disabilities Act (ADA), the Fair Labor Standards Act (FLSA), the Family and Medical Leave Act (FMLA), and the Health Insurance Portability and Accountability Act (HIPPA) among countless other employment laws and regulations.

You're well aware that a single violation of any one of those laws or regulations could cost you big time in court awarded judgments, fines, or both.

So . . . you work diligently, day in and day out, to keep your company out of court.

You know better than most what going to court can mean . . . *huge legal fees, key personnel bogged down in depositions and court appearances, lengthy delays, negative publicity, declining employee morale, and more* . . . with no guarantee that you'll win.

What more can you do to keep your company out of court?

You can make sure that senior management and key personnel keep up with the HR laws and regulations that can do serious damage to the economic stability of your company (something Walgreen's HR managers undoubtedly wish they had done just a few years ago before the company was forced to settle an employee discrimination lawsuit by paying $18.5 million to affected employees plus a payment of $5.5 million to the attorneys who sued Walgreen's in the first place).

While the specter of costly HR settlements is unnerving, it is important to remember that government agencies, not the least of which is the U.S. Equal Employment Opportunity Commission (EEOC), do not hesitate to levy huge fines against businesses that violate, knowingly or not, employee laws and regulations.

How can you keep up with all the local, state, and federal employment laws and regulations that can cripple your company's economic survival?

The best way, the surest way, to keep your company out of court is to educate senior managers and key personnel on how to manage the HR issues that make your company vulnerable.

And that means regularly schedule employment law training, on-site, off-site, in-house, or out-sourced . . . it's a simple and exceedingly necessary choice that bears repeating.

Doesn't it?

PART IV – EEOC RULINGS

Chapter 34
Who is the EEOC
and why should you care?

THOUGH I'VE GIVEN YOU A THUMBNAIL SKETCH OF the U.S. Equal Employment Opportunity Commission (EEOC) in Chapter 7 (page 24), you would be well advised to know as much as you can about the agency that may one day be an adversary.

So, let's take an in-depth look at America's primary employment law watchdog by quoting from the EEOC website (http://www.eeoc.gov).

It reads like this . . . the EEOC *"is responsible for enforcing federal laws that make it illegal to discriminate against a job applicant or an employee because of the person's race, color, religion, sex (including pregnancy), national origin, age (40 or older), disability or genetic information. It is also illegal to discriminate against a person because the person complained about discrimination, filed a charge of* discrimination, or participated in an employment discrimination investigation or lawsuit.

Most employers with at least 15 employees are covered by EEOC laws (20 employees in age discrimination cases). Most labor unions and employment agencies are also covered.

The laws apply to all types of work situations, including hiring, firing, promotions, harassment, training, wages, and benefits.

Authority & Role

The EEOC has the authority to investigate charges of discrimination against employers who are covered by the law. Our role in an investigation is to fairly and accurately assess the allegations in the charge and then make a finding. If we find that discrimination has occurred, we will try to settle the charge. If we aren't successful, we have the authority to file a lawsuit to protect the rights of individuals and the interests of the public. We do not, however, file lawsuits in all cases where we find discrimination.

We also work to prevent discrimination before it occurs through outreach, education and technical assistance programs.

The EEOC provides leadership and guidance to federal agencies on all aspects of the federal government's equal employment opportunity program. EEOC assures federal agency and department compliance with EEOC regulations, provides technical assistance to federal agencies concerning EEO complaint adjudication, monitors and evaluates federal agencies' affirmative employment programs, develops and distributes federal sector educational materials and conducts training for stakeholders, provides guidance and assistance to our Administrative Judges who conduct hearings on EEO complaints, and adjudicates appeals from administrative decisions made by federal agencies on EEO complaints.

Location

We carry out our work through our headquarters offices in Washington, D.C. and through 53 field offices serving every part of the nation."

I've decided to incorporate the following EEOC rulings to not only illustrate the types of employment law challenges faced by employers, large and small, but to also help you understand the scope of the EEOC's power and its standing in America's system of justice.

Chapter 35
Wal-Mart to pay $150,000 to settle EEOC age and disability discrimination suit

EEOC PRESS RELEASE - 2-19-15

Keller Store Manager Was Harassed and Fired Because of His Age and Denied Accommodation for His Diabetes, Federal Agency Charged

DALLAS - Wal-Mart Stores of Texas, L.L.C. (Wal-Mart) has agreed to pay $150,000 and provide other significant relief to settle an age and disability discrimination lawsuit brought by the U.S. Equal Employment Opportunity Commission (EEOC), the agency announced today. The EEOC charged in its suit that Wal-Mart discriminated against the manager of the Keller, Texas Walmart store by subjecting him to harassment, discriminatory treatment, and discharge because of his age. The EEOC also charged that Wal-Mart refused to provide a reasonable accommodation for the man's disability as federal law requires.

According to the EEOC's suit, David Moorman was ridiculed with frequent taunts from his direct supervisor, including "old man" and "old food guy." The EEOC further alleged that Wal-Mart ultimately fired Moorman because of his age. Such alleged conduct violates the Age Discrimination in Employment Act (ADEA), which prohibits discrimination on the basis of age 40 or older, including age-based harassment.

The EEOC's suit also alleged that Wal-Mart unlawfully refused Moorman's request for a reasonable accommodation for his diabetes. Following his diagnosis and on the advice of his doctor, Moorman requested reassignment to a store co-manager or assistant manager position. According to the suit, Wal-Mart refused to engage in the interactive process of discussing Moorman's requested accommodation, eventually rejecting his request. Under the Americans with Disabilities Act (ADA), Wal-Mart had an obligation to reasonably accommodate Moorman's disability.

The EEOC filed suit on March 12, 2014, (Case No. 3:14-cv-00908 in U.S. District Court for the Northern District of Texas, Dallas Division) after first attempting to reach a pre-litigation settlement through its conciliation process.

"Mr. Moorman was subjected to taunts and bullying from his supervisor that made his working conditions intolerable," said EEOC Senior Trial Attorney Joel Clark. "The EEOC remains committed to prosecuting the rights of workers through litigation in federal court."

Under the terms of the two-year consent decree settling the case, Wal-Mart will pay $150,000 in relief to Moorman. In addition, Wal-Mart agreed to provide training for employees on the ADA and the ADEA. The training will include an instruction on the kind of conduct that may constitute unlawful discrimination or harassment, as well as an instruction on Wal-Mart's procedures for handling requests for reasonable accommodations under the ADA. Wal-Mart will also report to the EEOC regarding its compliance with the consent decree and post a notice to employees about the settlement.

"The EEOC is pleased that Wal-Mart recognized the value of resolving this case without any further court action," said EEOC Dallas District Director Janet Elizondo.

The EEOC enforces federal laws prohibiting employment discrimination. Further information about the EEOC is available on its web site at www.eeoc.gov.

Epilogue: Even a mega-retailer like Wal-Mart can fail to train managers and HR personell to treat employees with dignity and respect. Moreover, the world's largest retailer allowed a culture of ridicule and vitriole to force at least one employee to file a complaint with the Equal Employment Opportunity Commission (EEOC).

If Wal-Mart had considered investing in a one-day on-site employment law seminar, this unfortunate incident would very likely never have happened.

I invite you to call 877-763-2752 or send an Email to info@hrcompliancetraining.net today to learn more about how you can avoid the costly, time-consuming consequences associated with any employment law violation.

Chapter 36
KMART will pay $102,048 to settle EEOC disability discrimination lawsuit

PRESS RELEASE - *1-27-15*

Major Retailer Refused to Hire Applicant Because Kidney Disease Precluded Urine Sample, Federal Agency Charged

BALTIMORE - Kmart Corporation, a leading national retailer, will pay $102,048 and provide significant equitable relief to settle a federal disability discrimination lawsuit, the U.S. Equal Employment Opportunity Commission (EEOC) announced today.

According to the lawsuit, after Kmart offered Lorenzo Cook a job at its Hyattsville, Md., store, Cook advised the hiring manager that he could not provide a urine sample for the company's mandatory pre-employment drug screening due to his kidney disease and dialysis. Cook requested a reasonable accommodation such as a blood test, hair test, or other drug test that did not require a urine sample, the EEOC charged.   Kmart refused to provide that alternative test and denied Cook employment because of his disability, according to the suit.

Such alleged conduct violates the Americans with Disabilities Act (ADA), which requires employers to provide reasonable accommodation, including during the application and hiring process, unless it can show it would be an undue hardship. The ADA also prohibits employers from refusing to hire individuals because of their disability.

The EEOC filed suit (*EEOC v. Kmart Corporation; Sears Holdings Management Corporation,* Civil Action No. 13-cv-02576) in U.S. District Court for the District of Maryland after first attempting to reach a pre-litigation settlement through its conciliation process.

In addition to providing $102,048 in monetary relief to Cook, the two-year consent decree resolving this lawsuit provides substantial equitable relief, including enjoining Kmart from taking adverse employment actions on the basis of disability and failing to provide a reasonable accommodation. Kmart is also revising its drug testing policies and forms to specify the availability of reasonable accommodation for applicants or employees in the company's drug testing processes. The decree also requires Kmart to provide training on the equal employment opportunity laws enforced by the EEOC, and on Kmart's ADA policy and the provision of reasonable accommodation, including as it relates to the company's drug testing processes. This training is required for all store managers, store assistant managers and human resources leads in the district where the alleged discrimination occurred. Kmart will also post a notice regarding the resolution of this lawsuit.

"There was a readily available alternative to the urinalysis test in this situation," said EEOC Philadelphia District Director Spencer H. Lewis, Jr. "This case demonstrates that the consequences of failing to comply with the ADA can be far more expensive than the actual cost of providing a reasonable accommodation."

EEOC Philadelphia Regional Attorney Debra M. Lawrence added, "We are pleased that this settlement compensates Mr. Cook for the harm he suffered and contains equitable relief designed to ensure that all employees and applicants with disabilities will receive equal employment opportunities, including reasonable accommodations as required by law."

The EEOC enforces federal laws prohibiting employment discrimination. Further information about the Commission is available at its website, www.eeoc.gov.

The Philadelphia District Office of the EEOC oversees Pennsylvania, Maryland, Delaware, West Virginia and parts of New Jersey and Ohio. The legal staff of the Philadelphia District Office of the EEOC also prosecutes discrimination cases arising from Washington, D.C. and parts of Virginia.

Epilogue: Another big name corporation bites the employment law dust, so to speak. Kmart, one of the most recognizable names in America, violated the Americans with Disabilities Act (ADA), hurt an innocent person, and spent an estimated quarter of a million dollars in monetary relief and legal fees because it failed to train a hiring manager in an urban Maryland location. The EEOC's lawsuit revealed that Kmart failed to provide employment law training to hiring managers, store managers, assistant store managers, and HR assistants in the district where this violation ostensibly occurred.

If Kmart had taken advantage of a one-day on-site employment law seminar, this unfortunate incident would likely never have happened.

I invite you to call 877-763-2752 or send an Email to info@hrcompliancetraining.net today to learn more about how you can avoid the costly, time-consuming consequences associated with any employment law violation.

Chapter 37
Citicorp ordered to pay nearly $340,000 for violating the Equal Pay Act

PRESS RELEASE – 4-16-2012

Citicorp service manager was paid substantially less than her male counterpart

TAMPA – When Heidi Wilson was promoted to a management position in the Tampa, Florida Citicorp service center in 2009, her annual salary was approximately $75,000.00 a year.

After 11 years of service, Wilson was terminated by Citicorp in 2011 and was denied severance pay and she responded by filing a lawsuit against Citicorp, claiming that Citicorp had violated the Equal Pay Act by failing to pay her the same salary as male managers in that same service center.

Evidence presented during the trial revealed that Wilson's predecessor in the Tampa service center management position had received an annual salary of nearly $130,000.00, some $55,000.00 more than Wilson was paid.

While Citicorp claimed in court documents that it compensates employees based on experience, merit, and seniority, the court found that the company typically paid male employees significantly larger salaries and bonuses than they paid to female employees, despite the effects of the Great Recession.

Wilson ultimately prevailed in her lawsuit against Citicorp and the court awarded her a one-time payment of nearly $340,000.00.

The EEOC enforces federal laws prohibiting employment discrimination. Further information about the EEOC is available on its web site at www.eeoc.gov.

Epilogue: Citicorp failed to follow the Equal Payment law and, as a result, paid a significant penalty in not only the court awarded $340,000.00 but also in lost productivity, attorney fees, and court costs.

If Citicorp had invested a tiny percentage point of their costs to defend the Heidi Wilson case in employment law training, this unfortunate incident may well never have happened.

Chapter 38
EEOC sues BNV Home Care Agency for violating Genetic Information Nondiscrimination Act

PRESS RELEASE - 9-17-14

BNV Home Care Agency unlawfully asked for genetic information from applicants and employees, federal agency charges

NEW YORK - BNV Home Care Agency, Inc., a New York City home care services agency which provides companionship and home care services for seniors, violated federal law when it asked applicants and employees for genetic information, the U.S. Equal Employment Opportunity Commission (EEOC) charged in a lawsuit filed today.

According to the EEOC's suit, BNV Home Care Agency asked for family medical history, a form of prohibited genetic information, from a class of thousands of applicants and employees through an "Employee Health Assessment" form. The form asked the applicant or employee to indicate any illnesses experienced by family members, including health conditions such as diabetes, kidney disease, heart disease, high blood pressure, arthritis, mental illness, epilepsy and cancer. BNV Home Care Agency required applicants to complete the form after offering them jobs but before hiring them and employees were required to complete the form on an annual basis after starting their jobs.

Such alleged conduct violates the Genetic Information Nondiscrimination Act (GINA) passed by Congress in 2008 and enforced by the EEOC. GINA prevents employers from re-questing genetic information, including family medical history, or using that information in the hiring process. The EEOC filed suit (Case No. 14-CV-5441) in U.S. District Court for the Eastern District of New York after first attempting to reach a pre-litigation settlement through its conciliation process.

"GINA is clear: employers cannot ask applicants or employees for their family medical history," said EEOC New York Regional Attorney Robert D. Rose. "The EEOC will pursue these cases to the fullest extent of the law to ensure that such genetic inquiries are never made of applicants or employees."

Konrad Batog, the trial attorney assigned to the case, added, "GINA has been in effect since 2009. Employers by now should have reviewed their procedures and practices to make sure that they or their agents do not violate the law by asking for family medical history."

The EEOC enforces federal laws prohibiting employment discrimination. Further information about the EEOC is available on its web site at www.eeoc.gov.

Epilogue: The BNV Home Care Agency case makes it clear to any employer who attempts to access the medical records of family members of any prospective or current employee that they are inviolating of the Genetic Information Nondiscrimination Act (GINA), a violation that could be costly in terms of lost productivity, attorney fees, and court costs.

Chapter 39
Seapod Pawnshops to pay $300,000 to settle EEOC harassment lawsuit

PRESS RELEASE - 2-12-15

Former Owner Harassed Employees Based on Sex, Race, and National Origin, and Fired Employees Who Filed Complaints, Federal Agency Charged

NEW YORK - Seapod Pawnbrokers, a chain of pawnshops in Brooklyn and Queens, N.Y., will pay $300,000 and cut ties with its former owner to settle an EEOC lawsuit charging harassment and retaliation against its Hispanic female employees, the agency announced today.

According to EEOC's lawsuit, Seapod's former owner and manager, Frank Morea, violated federal law when he harassed workers because of their sex, race and ethnicity, and fired workers who complained of the mistreatment. The EEOC said that Morea referred to the mostly Hispanic female workforce as "my Seapod bitches," regularly subjected them to graphic sexual comments, and referred to the women as his "whipping slaves." He also openly disparaged African-American customers, referring to them as "black bastards" and stating that the store smelled because "the monkeys are coming in." When employees resisted his sexual advances or complained about the harassment, he terminated them, the EEOC said.

Title VII of the Civil Rights Act of 1964 prohibits harassment based on sex, race, or national origin and retaliation against employees for resisting or making complaints about such harassment. The EEOC filed suit (*EEOC v. Seapod Pawnbrokers, Inc.*, d/b/a Seapod Pawnbrokers, and Seapod Capital Group, LLC, d/b/a Seapod Pawnbrokers, Case No. 14-CV-4567) in U.S. District Court for the Eastern District of New York after first attempting to reach a voluntary pre-litigation settlement through its conciliation process.

Today U.S. District Judge Kiyo A. Matsumoto signed the four-year consent decree resolving the case. In addition to the $300,000 in monetary damages to be paid to the victims, the decree bars Morea from having any association with the company and forbids him from entering the stores or contacting employees. The decree also requires Seapod to implement policy revisions that provide for adequate complaint and investigation procedures, to distribute the policy changes to employees, and to post a notice of this resolution. Seapod will provide annual anti-harassment and anti-retaliation training for all employees, and allow the EEOC to monitor its employment practices throughout the decree's four-year term.

"Too often, workers feel helpless when harassed by their higher-ups, especially vulnerable workers in low-wage jobs," said Robert D. Rose, regional attorney for the EEOC's New York District. "The EEOC will hold employers to account for their unlawful conduct, particularly when vulnerable workers are targeted."

Thomas Lepak, the EEOC trial attorney assigned to the case, added, "Thanks to the sweeping changes agreed to in this decree, Seapod's employees will no longer have to endure abuse and insult just to keep their jobs."

Targeting workplace harassment, particularly harassment of vulnerable populations, is of one of six national priorities identified by the EEOC's Strategic Enforcement Plan.

The New York District Office of the EEOC oversees New York, Northern New Jersey, Connecticut, Massachusetts, Rhode Island, Vermont, New Hampshire, and Maine.

Productivity and the Law
Louis Martin, JD
Productivity is a goal achieved only by contented employees

The EEOC is responsible for enforcing federal laws against employment discrimination. Further information is available at www.eeoc.gov.

Chapter 40
Swift Aviation to pay $50,000 to settle EEOC national origin and religious discrimination lawsuit

PRESS RELEASE - 7-29-13

Company Subjected Muslim Employee to Hateful and Derogatory Harassment, Federal Agency Charged

PHOENIX - Swift Aviation Services, Inc., a Phoenix aeronautical services company, will pay $50,000 and furnish other relief in order to settle a lawsuit filed by the U.S. Equal Employment Opportunity Commission (EEOC), the agency announced today.

The EEOC claimed in its suit that Swift Aviation violated federal law when it subjected former employee Adam Donmez to unlawful harassment because of his Turkish/Palestinian national origin and because he is Muslim. The alleged harassment included statements from supervisors such as, "I don't know why we don't just kill all them

149 |

towelheads"; asking Donmez why he was "dressed like [he was] gonna blow up the World Trade Center"; and derogatory jokes about Arabs. The EEOC also claimed that Donmez reported the harassment to another supervisor, but Swift Aviation failed to stop the harassment. Ultimately, the harassment was so bad that Donmez was forced to resign his employment, according to the EEOC.

Harassment based on national origin or religion violates Title VII of the Civil Rights Act of 1964. The EEOC filed suit (*EEOC v. Swift Aviation Group, et al*, Case No. 2:12-cv-01867-MHB in U.S. District Court for the District of Arizona) after first attempting to reach a voluntary settlement through its conciliation process. The consent decree settling this case, which was entered on July 24, 2013, requires Swift Aviation to provide $50,000 in monetary relief to Donmez, including back wages and compensatory damages. The decree also permanently prohibits Swift Aviation from subjecting any employee to harassment or retaliation based on national origin or religion, and requires the company to provide training to its managers and employees and to notify the EEOC about future harassment complaints.

"Today's settlement serves as a message to employers that national origin and religious discrimination is a violation of federal law and will not be tolerated," said

150 |

Regional Attorney Mary Jo O'Neill of the EEOC's Phoenix District Office. "Employers have obligations to their employees, and when employers choose not to meet those obligations, the EEOC is prepared to pursue all appropriate means to hold them accountable."

Rayford O. Irvin, director of the EEOC's Phoenix District Office, added, "This action shows the EEOC's unwavering commitment to eradicating national origin and religious discrimination in the workplace. We are pleased that an agreement could be reached this early in the litigation."

Swift Aviation is a commercial business at Phoenix Sky Harbor International Airport that provides aeronautical services such as the fueling and hangaring of aircraft and aircraft maintenance. The company is incorporated in Arizona.

Epilogue: Harassment of Muslims in the workplace typically occurs when colleagues don't understand the Muslim culture and religion and therefore assume that Muslims (those who practice the Islam religion) are terrorists. An understanding of Islam and Islamic practices reveals that the majority of Muslims refute terrorism. If Swift Aviation management had engaged an employment law trainer who understood the depth and breadth of anti-Muslim tensions in Swift Aviation's workforce, this case could have been prevented.

Chapter 41
Savi Technology will pay $20,000 to settle EEOC pregnancy discrimination lawsuit

PRESS RELEASE - 3-2-15

Company Rescinded Job Offer to Applicant One Day After Learning She Had Recently Given Birth, Federal Agency Charges

ALEXANDRIA, Va. - Savi Technology, Inc., an Alexandria, Va.-headquartered provider of sensor-based analytics, software and hardware, will pay $20,000 and furnish significant remedial relief to settle a federal pregnancy discrimination lawsuit filed by the U.S. Equal Employment Opportunity Commission (EEOC), the agency announced today.

The EEOC charged that Savi offered Christine Rowe a job as the director of human resources, but the company rescinded the job offer one day after it learned that she had recently given birth and had surgery related to her pregnancy.

Such conduct violates Title VII of the Civil Rights Act of 1964, as amended by the Pregnancy Discrimination Act, which prohibits discrimination on the basis of pregnancy, childbirth or related medical conditions. The EEOC filed suit (*EEOC v. Savi Technology, Inc.*, Civil Action No.1:14-cv-1005) in the U.S. District Court for the Eastern District of Virginia, Alexandria Division, after first attempting to reach a voluntary pre-litigation settlement through its conciliation process.

In addition to the $20,000 in monetary relief to Rowe, the two-year consent decree resolving the lawsuit precludes Savi from taking adverse employment actions on the basis of pregnancy in the future. Savi will distribute its EEO policy, which prohibits sex and pregnancy discrimination, to all employees. The company will provide annual EEO training to all of its U.S. employees and post a notice regarding the settlement. Savi will also report to the EEOC on its compliance with the consent decree, including how it handled complaints of alleged pregnancy discrimination.

"Unfortunately, pregnancy discrimination is still a pervasive problem in the workplace," said EEOC Washington Field Office Acting Director Mindy Weinstein. "Employers would be wise to review the Commission's recent enforcement guidance on pregnancy discrimination to ensure that they do not engage in unlawful actions when making employment decisions."

EEOC Philadelphia District Office Regional Attorney Debra M. Lawrence added, "The injunctive relief and training provisions in the consent decree are designed to prevent pregnancy discrimination. No woman should be denied a job because of her pregnancy or because she recently gave birth. We are pleased that Savi Technology worked with us to resolve this lawsuit quickly."

According to company information, Savi specializes in providing sensor-based predictive analytic solutions that enable customers to track and monitor high value assets.

The Commission recently issued Enforcement Guidance on Pregnancy Discrimination and Related Issues, along with a question and answer document about the guidance and a fact sheet for small businesses. **Enforcement Guidance, Q&A document, and Fact Sheet are available on the EEOC website.**

The EEOC's Washington Field Office has jurisdiction over the District of Columbia and the State of Virginia Counties of Arlington, Clarke, Fairfax, Fauquier, Frederick, Loudoun, Prince William, Stafford, and Warren; and the State of Virginia Independent Cities of Alexandria, Fairfax City, Falls Church, Manassas, Manassas Park, and Winchester. The legal staff of the EEOC's Philadelphia District Office prosecutes discrimination cases arising from Pennsylvania, Maryland, Delaware, West Virginia, Washington, D.C., and parts of New Jersey, Ohio, and Virginia.

Chapter 42
Kauai County in Hawaii settles EEOC race harassment case for $120,000

PRESS RELEASE - 9-6-12

White County Attorney Subjected to Racially Disparaging Remarks by Top-Level Manager, Federal Agency Charged

HONOLULU - The County of Kauai in Hawaii will pay $120,000 to settle a federal charge of race harassment filed with the U.S. Equal Employment Opportunity Commission (EEOC), the federal agency announced today.

A former attorney for the County of Kauai's Office of the Prosecuting Attorney since 2009 filed the EEOC charge of discrimination in 2010, prompting an investigation by the federal agency. The former attorney, who is white, alleged that she was harassed due to her race by a top-level manager. The manager allegedly made continually disparaging comments to the former attorney, saying that she needed to assimilate more into the local culture and break up with her boyfriend at the time, also white, in favor of a local boy.

The EEOC ultimately found reasonable cause to believe that the county violated Title VII of the Civil Rights Act of 1964 for the harassment to which the former attorney was subjected. Following the determination, the County of Kauai entered into an over two-year conciliation agreement with the EEOC and the alleged victim. The agreement effectively settles the case administratively, thereby avoiding potential litigation. Aside from the monetary relief, the county agreed to establish policies and complaint procedures dealing with discrimination and harassment in the workplace and to provide live EEO training to all managers and supervisors. The county further agreed to post notices on the matter on all bulletin boards throughout the county and to permit the disclosure of the settlement.

"The workplace is no place for derogatory remarks pertaining to race or any other protected basis, and it is important for an employer to take immediate corrective action when faced with illegal harassment," said Timothy Riera, director of the EEOC's Honolulu Local Office. "We commend the County of Kauai for expeditiously resolving this matter and agreeing to measures which will prevent and deal with both harassment and discrimination on the job."

The County of Kauai's Office of the Prosecuting Attorney is a local government agency responsible for criminal prosecution under the laws of the state of Hawaii and the ordinances, rules and regulations of the county of Kauai.

The EEOC enforces federal laws prohibiting employment discrimination. More information about the EEOC is available on its web site at www.eeoc.gov.

Chapter 43
Kentucky Fried Chicken franchise pays $40,000 to settle EEOC religious discrimination lawsuit

PRESS RELEASE - 12-23-13

Laurinburg Companies Unlawfully Fired Pentecostal Employee for Refusing to Wear Pants, Federal Agency Charged

LAURINBURG, N.C. - Scottish Food Systems, Inc. and Laurinburg KFC Take Home, Inc. will pay $40,000 and furnish other relief to resolve a religious discrimination lawsuit filed by the U.S. Equal Employment Opportunity Commission (EEOC), the agency announced today. Scottish Food Systems and Laurinburg KFC Take Home are based in Laurinburg, N.C. and jointly operate a chain of Kentucky Fried Chicken restaurants in North Carolina.

According to the EEOC's complaint, Sheila Silver converted to Pentecostalism in 2010. As a member of the

Pentecostal church, Silver believes women cannot wear pants. In accordance with this religious belief, Silver has not worn pants since the fall of 2010. Silver has worked for various Kentucky Fried Chicken restaurants since 1992. Scottish Food Systems and Laurinburg KFC Take Home purchased the KFC restaurant where Silver worked in Rocky Mount, N.C., in April 2013. The EEOC's complaint alleged that the companies informed Silver she must wear pants to work because of their dress code policy. According to the EEOC, Silver told Scottish Food Systems and Laurinburg KFC Take Home she could not wear pants because of her religious beliefs. However, the companies ultimately fired her for refusing to wear pants to work.

Such alleged conduct violates Title VII of the Civil Rights Act of 1964 (Title VII), which requires employers to reasonably accommodate an employee's religious beliefs as long as doing so would not pose an undue hardship. The EEOC filed suit on September 19, 2013 in U.S. District Court for the Middle District of North Carolina (*EEOC v. Scottish Food Systems, Inc. and Laurinburg KFC Take Home, Inc.*, Civil Action No. 1:13-CV-00796) after first attempting to reach a pre-litigation settlement through its conciliation process.

In addition to monetary damages, the three-year consent decree resolving the suit requires Scottish Food

Systems and Laurinburg KFC Take Home to adopt a formal religious accommodation policy and to conduct an annual training program on the requirements of Title VII and its prohibition against religious discrimination. Scottish Food Systems and Laurinburg KFC Take Home will also post a copy of their anti-discrimination policy at all of their facilities.

"Employers must accommodate an employee's sincerely held religious belief when such an accommodation would not pose an undue hardship," said Lynette A. Barnes, regional attorney for the EEOC's Charlotte District Office. "This case demonstrates the EEOC's continued commitment to fighting religious discrimination in the workplace."

The EEOC is responsible for enforcing federal laws prohibiting discrimination in employment. Additional information about the EEOC is available at www.eeoc.gov

Chapter 44
Jury awards $499,000
against EmCare in EEOC sexual
harassment and retaliation case

PRESS RELEASE - 10-27-14

Physician Outsourcing Group Fired Employees for Reporting Sexually Charged Environment, Jury Found

DALLAS - A Dallas federal court jury, on Friday, October 24, 2014, returned a verdict awarding almost half a million dollars to three former employees in a sexual harassment and retaliation lawsuit by the U.S. Equal Employment Opportunity Commission against EmCare, a provider of physician services, the federal agency announced.

The jury of two women and four men awarded former Executive Assistant Gloria Stokes $250,000 in punitive damages based on the claim that she was sexually harassed by her supervisor, the division CEO, Jim McKinney. Stokes, who filed a discrimination charge with the EEOC, also

162 |

individually intervened in the Commission's lawsuit and was personally represented by Laura Hallmon of Fielding, Parker & Hallmon LLP. The case was tried before U.S. District Judge Jorge Solis.

The EEOC also sought relief for Bonnie Shaw, an EmCare credentialer, and Luke Trahan, a recruiter, based on retaliatory discharge. The jury awarded Shaw and Trahan $82,000 and $167,000, respectively, to compensate them for lost wages and benefits as a result of having been fired for reporting and opposing a sexually hostile work environment within the AnesthesiaCare Division of EmCare.

The jury verdict followed five days of trial, including the presentation of evidence by the EEOC about constant lewd sexual comments and behavior of former AnesthesiaCare CEO Jim McKinney, as well as several other management-level employees in that Division. Stokes, Shaw and Trahan all testified about the lack of an appropriate response by Human Resources to their complaints about the misconduct. Shaw and Trahan testified about jointly reporting to human resources that McKinney made an inappropriate remark to Shaw's then-15-year-old daughter at a "Bring Your Child to Work Day" event. Shaw and Trahan were both fired, within an hour of each other, just six weeks later for reasons the company alleged were performance issues.

Sexual harassment and retaliation for complaining about it violate Title VII of the Civil Rights Act of 1964. The EEOC filed suit (Civil Action No. 3:11-CV-02017-P) in U.S. District Court for the Northern District of Texas after first attempting to reach a pre-litigation settlement through its conciliation process.

"Ms. Stokes, Ms. Shaw, and Mr. Trahan spent their time at EmCare working diligently to do their jobs well despite the pervasive sexual environment that human resources allowed Jim McKinney to create and perpetuate," said EEOC Senior Trial Attorney Meaghan Shepard. "Their complaints were ignored, and instead of getting support from HR, Ms. Shaw and Mr. Trahan were fired for daring to speak out against the division CEO. By today's verdict, it is clear that all three have finally been heard."

EEOC General Counsel David Lopez added, "The EEOC stands ready to take cases to the people through the courthouse, and to shine light on these stories of discrimination and retaliation whenever early administrative resolutions cannot be reached. It is particularly important for us to act to protect employees who have risked their jobs simply because they have stepped up to challenge discrimination in the workplace."

Janet Elizondo, director of the EEOC's Dallas District Office, said, "I am very pleased with the excellent work of our investigative staff in preparing the case that led to this great result. Retired EEOC Investigator Norma Warner returned to provide rebuttal testimony that I'm sure was critical in helping this jury reach its decision."

EmCare has more than 750 practices serving nearly 600 hospitals, hospital systems and other healthcare facilities nationwide.

The EEOC is responsible for enforcing federal laws against employment discrimination. For more information about the agency, go to www.eeoc.gov.

Chapter 45
Ventura Corporation to pay $354,250 to settle EEOC lawsuit for sex discrimination against men

PRESS RELEASE - 4-3-14

Federal agency charged beauty wholesaler with refusing to hire men and retaliating against a manager who opposed the discrimination

MIAMI - Ventura Corporation, a Puerto Rico-based wholesaler of makeup, beauty products, jewelry and other personal care items to retail sellers, has agreed to settle a sex discrimination lawsuit filed by the U.S. Equal Employment Opportunity Commission (EEOC), the agency announced today.

The EEOC charged in its suit that Ventura engaged in a pattern or practice of refusing to hire men as Zone Managers and Support Managers. The EEOC also alleged that Ventura promoted Erick Zayas into a Zone Manager position after he complained about its discriminatory practices, only to set him up for failure and termination in retaliation for his opposition to Ventura's sex-based hiring practices.

Sex discrimination and retaliation violate Title VII of the Civil Rights Act of 1964. The EEOC filed suit (Case No. 3:11-cv-01700-PG) in U.S. District Court for Puerto Rico after first investigating the case, and then attempting to reach a pre-litigation settlement through its conciliation process.

According to the terms of the consent decree settling the suit, which was approved by the court on March 27, 2014, Ventura will pay $354,250 to settle the lawsuit, including a payment to Zayas of $150,000. The remaining settlement funds will be paid into an account that will be distributed to a class of qualified male job applicants who applied for Zone or Support Manager jobs with Ventura from 2004 to the present, but whom Ventura did not consider for hire. The agreement also requires Ventura to implement a detailed applicant tracking system; actively promote supervisory accountability for discrimination prevention; provide anti-discrimination training to all company employees and anti-discrimination training specific to those Ventura managers and employees who play a role in the hiring process; and provide bi-annual hiring reports to the EEOC for three years.

The EEOC said that the company was responsible for the loss or destruction of a great deal of critical evidence supporting the case. The disappeared evidence included job applications from qualified male applicants for the positions at issue and e-mails from key decision makers. The EEOC asked the court to award sanctions against the company based on the apparent destruction of evidence. The judge, agreeing with the EEOC's position, made a ruling that if the case were to proceed to a jury trial, he would instruct the jurors that they may draw an adverse inference from the vanished evidence, and may assume that it would have supported the EEOC's case regarding the company's violations of discrimination law.

"This case is another reminder that federal law protects both men and women from gender discrimination," said Robert E. Weisberg, regional attorney for the EEOC's Miami District Office. "We are pleased that we have been able to secure relief not only for Mr. Zayas, but also for the many qualified applicants who were not considered by Ventura for employment simply because they were male."

Malcolm Medley, director of the EEOC's Miami District Office, added, "There is no protection in the law for reliance on outdated sex stereotypes. When they appear in the workplace, employees must be able to raise legitimate concerns of discrimination without fear of retaliation."

The EEOC is responsible for enforcing federal laws against employment discrimination. The Miami District Office's jurisdiction includes Florida, Puerto Rico and U.S. Virgin Islands. Further information is available at www.eeoc.gov.

Chapter 46
Jury awards more than $1.5 million in EEOC sexual harassment and retaliation suit against New Breed Logistics

PRESS RELEASE - 5-10-13

MEMPHIS, Tenn. - A jury has rendered a verdict of more than $1.5 million in the U.S. Equal Employment Opportunity Commission's (EEOC) sexual harassment and retaliation lawsuit against New Breed Logistics, a North Carolina-based logistics services provider, the agency announced today. The verdict followed a seven-day trial before U.S. District Court Judge S. Thomas Anderson on behalf of four claimants and included awards of $177,094 in back pay, $486,000 in compensatory damages and $850,000 in punitive damages for the discrimination victims.

The EEOC's lawsuit charged New Breed Logistics with subjecting three female employees in Memphis to sexual harassment and retaliating against the three female employees and one male employee for opposing the harassment in violation of Title VII. Specifically, the jury found that New Breed, through the conduct of a warehouse supervisor, harassed three temporary workers by subjecting them to unwelcome sexual touching and lewd, obscene and vulgar sexual remarks at the company's Avaya Memphis area warehouse facility.

Further, the EEOC charged and the jury found, a New Breed supervisor fired the three temp workers because they complained about the harassment. In addition, the EEOC said, the supervisor also retaliated against a male employee by terminating him because he opposed the harassment and agreed to serve as a witness for several claimants during the company's investigation.

Sexual harassment and retaliation for complaining about it violate Title VII of the Civil Rights Act of 1964. The EEOC filed suit (Civil Action No. 2:10-cv-02696-STA-tmp) in U.S. District Court for the Western District of Tennessee at Memphis after first attempting to reach a voluntary settlement.

In addition to the monetary damages awarded by the jury totaling $1,513,094, the EEOC also seeks an injunction prohibiting discrimination in the future by the defendant as well as other injunctive relief to be determined by the court.

"This agency always works to resolve cases informally whenever possible," said EEOC General Counsel David Lopez. "When we are unable to do so, as we have demonstrated yet again, we will try the case to verdict to ensure that employers will be held accountable for discriminatory practices, including sexual harassment, and retaliation against individuals who oppose such misconduct. The EEOC has successfully tried eight cases during this fiscal year prevailing in all but one."

This jury verdict represents the second $1.5 million-dollar verdict in a sexual harassment case that the Memphis Office has obtained since March 2011.

Faye A. Williams, regional attorney for the Memphis District Office, said, "Memphis is often called 'America's Distribution Center.' Temporary employees, as were the claimants in this case, are a vital part of the country's work force, helping businesses to distribute goods across the United States and the world in a timely and efficient manner. Enduring sexual harassment by a supervisor should not be a part of the job. We hope this case and this verdict serve to remind employers of their responsibility to protect temporary employees placed in their facilities to work. Employers at the job site must provide a safe place for employees, including providing a sexual harassment policy to the workers, conducting training in the workplace about the policy and timely investigating claims of harassment."

New Breed Logistics, a logistics services provider that helps companies design and operate supply chains, warehousing and distribution, operates five Memphis warehouses. New Breed is a national company, headquartered in High Point, N.C. The company also has warehouses in Atlanta, Chicago, Dallas, Texas, Los Angeles and Kearny, N.J.

Further information about the EEOC is available on its web site at www.eeoc.gov.

Chapter 47
After 44 years, sheet metal union finally agrees to pay an estimated $12 million in partial settlement of race bias lawsuit

PRESS RELEASE – 4-2-15

EEOC and Others Charged Local 28 with Discriminating Against Black and Hispanic Workers for Many Years

NEW YORK - Subject to approval by the U.S. District Court for the Southern District of New York, Local 28 of the Sheet Metal Workers' International Association, the trade union for sheet metal journeypersons in New York City, has agreed to create a back pay fund for a group of minority sheet metal workers in partial settlement of race discrimination claims against the local union. Pursuant to the settlement, it is estimated that the union will pay approximately $12.7 million over the next five years and provide substantial remedial relief to partially resolve claims made against the union by the

U.S. Equal Employment Opportunity Commission (EEOC) and others, the agency announced today. The settlement was achieved after extensive negotiations with the union by the EEOC, the New York State Division of Human Rights, the City of New York, and a class of black and Hispanic union members represented by Debevoise & Plimpton LLP and the Lawyers' Committee for Civil Rights Under Law. A hearing is set for July 14 for the court to consider approving the proposed settlement.

Over the 44-year history of this case, the federal district court issued a number of rulings that Local 28 discriminated against non-white journeypersons on the basis of race, in violation of Title VII of the Civil Rights Act of 1964. The current settlement covers claims of work-hour disparities based on race for the 15-year period between April 1, 1991 and June 30, 2006. This settlement supplements a 2008 settlement of $6.2 million that covered back pay claims from January 1, 1984 through March 31, 1991.

The lawsuit (*EEOC, et al., v. Local 28 of the Sheet Metal Workers' Int'l Ass'n, et al.*, Case No. 71 Civ. 2887 (LAK)) was filed initially in 1971 in the U.S. District Court for the Southern District of New York by the Civil Rights Division of the Department of Justice, the New York State Division of Human

Rights, and the City of New York. The EEOC replaced the Department of Justice as prosecuting counsel in 1974.

Pursuant to the settlement, Local 28 will initially pay over $4 million in damages to journeypersons harmed by the discrimination and then contribute additional millions to a settlement fund over the next five years. The plaintiffs estimate that total payments will reach about $12.7 million, assuming that work levels remain at or near recent levels. Judge Lewis A. Kaplan will hold a Fairness Hearing regarding approval of the settlement on July 14, 2015 at 4:30 p.m. As part of the settlement, Local 28 also agreed to comprehensive reforms designed to equalize work opportunities for non-white and white union members. These include improved monitoring and investigation of discrimination complaints, an expansion of the use of the union's referral hall to guarantee non-discriminatory hiring decisions, increased education and training opportunities for members, and increased monitoring, analysis, and reporting of potential work-hours disparities by the union to EEOC and other plaintiffs.

"I am pleased that we have been able to negotiate this partial settlement that includes strong injunctive relief as well as individual relief," said EEOC General Counsel David Lopez. "This case demonstrates EEOC's longstanding commitment to achieving equal access to jobs regardless of race."

EEOC New York Regional Attorney Robert D. Rose said, "This partial settlement of EEOC's longstanding litigation against Local 28, if approved, is a big step forward for black and Hispanic sheet metal workers. The EEOC will continue to enforce the court orders in this case until full and lasting equality for those workers is realized."

"We are pleased that the Court will have a hearing in July on the proposed back pay settlement, and we are hopeful that the class members will soon be able to receive long-awaited compensation for past inequities in work allocation. We are also hopeful that the enhanced injunctive measures ordered by the Court will help to promote a more fair distribution of work opportunities in the future," said Wendy B. Reilly, counsel at Debevoise & Plimpton LLP.

Barbara Arnwine, President and Executive Director of the Lawyers' Committee for Civil Rights Under Law, added that, "We are pleased with the results, which are a testament to the unstinting efforts contributed by all counsel, particularly the attorneys at Debevoise & Plimpton who have served as our co-counsel for the class. This proposed settlement reflects the beneficial results that can be achieved for victims of discrimination when the private bar joins forces with government enforcement agencies, as the Lawyers' Committee has been doing for over 50 years."

"The proposed settlement, if approved, will be a major step forward in what has been a decades-long process to end discrimination against Black and Hispanic members of Local 28 and restore their lost wages," said Joshua Rubin, Senior Counsel at the New York City Law Department. "We will continue working to ensure that Local 28 adopts and maintains good practices at the union going forward so that all of its members are treated fairly, regardless of race or ethnicity."

More information about the EEOC is available on its web site at www.eeoc.gov.

Appendix – The major federal employment laws

YOUR HR MANAGEMENT TEAM is responsible for making sure that your entire workforce is safe, secure, and happy.

Big job.

Trying to keep a variety of personalities safe, secure, and happy in various jobs with various levels of responsibility requires thoughtful, sensible company policies that support compliance with a long list of complex federal employment laws and regulations.

The Department of Labor (DOL) and the Equal Employment Opportunity Commission (EEOC) investigate, prosecute, and enforce employment laws, including but not limited to:

- Black Lung Benefits Act (BLBA)
- Consumer Credit Protection Act (CCPA)
- Contract Work Hours and Safety Standards Act (CWHSSA)

- Copeland "Anti-Kickback" Act
- Davis-Bacon and Related Acts (DBRA)
- Employee Polygraph Protection Act (EPPA)
- Employee Retirement Income Security Act (ERISA)
- Energy Employees Occupational Illness Compensation Program Act (EEOICPA)
- Executive Order 11246
- Fair Labor Standards Act (FLSA)
- Family and Medical Leave Act (FMLA)
- Federal Employees' Compensation Act (FECA)
- Federal Mine Safety and Health Act (Mine Act)
- Immigration and Nationality Act (INA)
- Labor-Management Reporting and Disclosure Act (LMRDA)
- Longshore and Harbor Workers' Compensation Act (LHWCA)
- Mass Transit Employee Protections
- McNamara-O'Hara Service Contract Act (SCA)
- Migrant and Seasonal Agricultural Worker Protection Act (MSPA)
- Occupational Safety and Health (OSH) Act
- Rehabilitation Act of 1973, Section 503

- Sections 102 and 103 of the Civil Rights Act of 1991
- Sections 501 and 505 of the Rehabilitation Act of 1973
- The Age Discrimination in Employment Act of 1967 (ADEA)
- The Equal Pay Act of 1963 (EPA)
- The Genetic Information Nondiscrimination Act of 2008 (GINA)
- The Lily Ledbetter Pay Act of 2009
- The Pregnancy Discrimination Act
- Title I of the Americans with Disabilities Act of 1990 (ADA)
- Title VII of the Civil Rights Act of 1964 (Title VII)
- Uniformed Services Employment and Reemployment Rights Act (USERRA)
- Vietnam Era Veterans' Readjustment Assistance Act (VEVRAA)
- Walsh-Healey Public Contracts Act (PCA)
- Whistleblower Protections
- Worker Adjustment and Retraining Notification Act (WARN)

Productivity is a goal achieved only by contented employees

Louis Martin, JD